FUNDAMENTALS FOR SUCCESSFUL AND SUSTAINABLE FASHION BUYING AND MERCHANDISING

Charles Nesbitt

Copyright and ISBN page

Contents

8

FUNDAMENTALS FOR SUCCESSFUL AND SUSTAINABLE FASHION BUYING AND MERCHANDISING

PREFACE

The process of buying and selling in some form or other of goods has been with us since time immemorial. Often when one stands in bewilderment in an elegant shopping mall and wonder how all the stores are able to effectively seduce the many shoppers trawling the wide corridors to readily part with their well-earned money while at the same time enabling them to possibly enjoy a wonderful social experience.

The plan of offering goods to the potential customer is a complicated one and is a science that involves many players whose individual contributions slot seamlessly together and are so perfectly co-ordinated that it provides the perception that it is the result of one individual concerted effort.

It will be illustrated as to how the relationships of the major functions that intertwine from the conceptualisation of a product through to the presentation of a finished garment to the potential customer and in doing this demonstrates how the key areas such as buying, merchandising, technology, production, design, logistics and selling each with their unique specialised operations manage to achieve this.

The book endeavours to try and outline the basic key principles and mechanisms by which this happens and should be helpful to students, people in retailing and those who are maybe considering a career in the industry. For those who already are part of the fashion buying and merchandising community this book will be beneficial in that it provides a complete simplified overview of all the integral activities and roles that go to make up the topic and thereby will provide a broader insight into their own career.

The material of the book, other than that specifically referenced is the result of the author's own exposure to the subject during a career spanning thirty five years at a major retail organisation in Southern Africa, the support from colleagues, mentors, interaction with suppliers and own research. There has been some cross referencing to other books or technical material but the book focuses largely at a higher level on the key principles, concepts and theories and hence there is none or very little mention of retailers by name or technological packages for some key activities such as planning, allocating, critical path management, logistics and the like.

The fundamental purpose is therefore to provide the basic background that goes into the operational and technical aspects which can be universally applied. While there is merit and great benefits in the use of sophisticated technical packages that live off a common database and also integrate with one another, sadly often the prime emphasis becomes more one of mastering the system and promotes the tendency to live in a silo environment. As a result the importance tends to be focused on that single facet that the system serves rather than the broader picture. The fact that there is a relatively limited amount of material that generally describes the practice commonly known as retailing as an end to end process considering the enormous size of the industry is one of the motivating reasons for the documentation of this book.

INTRODUCTION

Retailing

Retailing is the offer of goods or services for sale by individuals or businesses to an end user. The channels by which these goods reach the final user may vary considerably and arrive via different sources such as wholesalers, trading houses or directly from the manufacturer and there are equally many differing variants in the way the goods are put on sale. Historically it is more likely that shopping would have been done at the village or town market, in a high street shop or at the "mom and pop" store which evolved over time into mass retailing stores that are often housed in shopping malls supported by smaller line shops.

More recently with the advent of the computer utilising various platforms such as the internet or social networks, shopping on line is growing exponentially using electronic payment methods with delivery via the post or with a courier man knocking on the front door of the customer bearing their purchase relatively shortly after the transaction has been processed.

The products that are put on offer will be determined by the demand to satisfy a need in the market place. Broadly the merchandise may be categorized into food stuffs, hard or durable goods such as appliances, furniture and electronics and soft goods that have a limited life span typically clothing, apparel and fabrics. Whatever the nature of the product, the key objective will be to acquire and sell the product at a price that will be more than it cost to bring it to the place of offer and thereby make a profit.

Supporting activities such as the storage, movement of the goods, technology, and marketing will endeavour to ensure that the form, function and profit objective is maximised.

The retail players

The saying "no man is an island" holds true in many spheres and this is certainly the case in the world of clothing retailing.

Various players, each with very different specialised skills are amalgamated together to deliver a completed outcome which is that of presenting product for sale to potential customers. These players are often very diverse not only in the activities that they perform but also in their personality traits which they possess. The key to a successful team is how maturely the interaction takes place and the mutual respect that every member has for each other's roles.

Below is a brief synopsis of the main player's roles and their dependency and integration with each other. The intimate details of the roles will be exposed in the future chapters as the science of retailing is explored in greater detail.

THE PROCUREMENT TEAM

The foremost players in the clothing and apparel procurement team consist typically of the following members and are described in broad terms.

Designers

Designers have a deep insight into the market they are targeting through the analysis of the changing trends and use these to provide creative direction and develop product designs for the buying teams to consider.

Usually these participants tend to think out of the box and their creative minds can challenge some of the comfort zones of other team members. What must be kept top of mind is that they need to consistently apply their intellect way ahead of time as to what they think the customer requires as opposed to their personal desires.

Typically the character traits which they will possess are that they are independent, spontaneous, extroverts, driven by ideas and are confident by nature.

Although the general perception of the word "designer" conjures up a vision of those who work at couture level, the reality is that it also includes those who are involved in creating ranges which may also be exclusive but will be more widely available and therefore can be considered as having been mass produced. Their choices will be influenced by the type of retailer they work for or the product category that they design for. The more traditional retailer which serves predominantly mature customers will be less influenced by radical fashion swings which in contrast will definitely affect the younger market's high fashion boutiques more rigorously.

Work is done at times under enormous pressure to meet critical deadlines, tough meeting schedules and involves frequent international travel. It is not surprising the perception is often one that they live a life of glory and glamour but contrary to this belief the reality is that it is not as extravagant as made out to be.

The fashion and trade shows, whether they be for yarn, fabric or garments are tiring affairs requiring hard work and stamina as is the shopping for appropriate samples, researching fashion magazines, the use of forecasting trend agencies, internet and blogs and out of all of this they need to possess the ability to then distil the emerging trends to create a storybook that will best suit their organisation's customer profiles.

The designer lives with the constant strain of knowing that their level of success will be measured by the eventual amount of money rung up at the till and getting the styling direction wrong or overextending the life of a particular look could have severe financial implications, especially in the cases where volumes are high.

The real challenge is to convince the buying teams and senior management to buy into their vision and have the confidence that what they have in mind will be commercially acceptable to the customer. The designer cannot ignore the technical aspects of the garment production as many problems can be evaded if these are taken cognisance of during the design process.

Retailers in the southern hemisphere do have the advantage that their seasons follow those of countries in the northern hemisphere which allows them to tap into the more successful designs that are trading in volume. However, with globalisation this is not always as clear cut as it was in previous years and the ability to follow as close to the season as possible requires techniques that facilitates the shortening of lead times and attempt to get the product to market as quickly as possible. The advent of communication technologies such as satellite television, internet and social media have brought exposure to different cultures, sports, films, lifestyles and trends such as those generated by specific events, health drives, environmental awareness and technology platforms that can have significant impacts on fashion which sometimes happen at very short notice.

A very important aspect is that the designer must adhere strictly to, is that of copyright. Instances have occurred that other competitor's garments are copied almost identically whether it be by style, print or design. Invariably the driving reason for this is the speed of being able to turn on a replica at a cheaper price. Although it may not be practical to register and copyright every design, any infringement can still be challenged and a consequence could occur of having the offending garments being removed from display and destroyed.

Buyers

The buyer needs to have a clear understanding of the product that is required which is in line with the trend guidelines best suited to their target customer profiles, for both the high fashion segment as well as those that best serve the more traditional customer.

It is a fact is that the role of the designer and the buyer may be a bit blurred in that they research the same fashion forecasting sites and other sources of inspiration in order to put a range of garments together. Both roles must be aware of sizing, quality and costs related to fabrics, trimmings and production. To achieve this successfully they must be flexible enough to develop and buy the most suitable product that is in line with the prescribed strategy and achieves the desired profit margin in keeping with the set down targets. The evaluation of competitive activity and product ranges through regular store visits and comparative shopping provides the knowledge required to keep ahead of the field.

Effective communication and presentation skills are a prerequisite to brief and interact with suppliers as well as presenting product reviews to colleagues within their own group at all levels of seniority. With this comes the need to be able to accept criticism and resolve problems in a mature manner. The sad fact is that frequently when the analysis of the success of the range is evaluated at the end of the season, if the results are disappointing it is not uncommon for the buyer to shoulder the emotional burden of the poor performance. The truth of the matter is that the range was presented on more than one occasion to all team players including senior management all of whom signed the range off but in the final analysis they are more often than not, as is human nature, reluctant to be accept any proper accountability.

Coupled to ability to understand the wants of the customer is the sourcing of the most suitable supplier that will be selected for the specified product types in terms of their particular skills, technical ability, costing efficiency, attitude, transparency, honesty, focus on quality, communications and competitiveness while still meeting the ethical criteria that are acceptable to society.

A large part of the task will be to maintain good relations with suppliers, while at the same time being able to assertively negotiate prices with them and make sure the planned stocks are delivered on time. Communications need to be clear and specific to avoid disputes over issues which may arise through vague and confusing messages. For these reasons they need to be confident, take decisions based on results and be driven by a sense of urgency.

The buyer has to be multi-talented in that as well as being creative they also need to monitor the sales objectively and be flexible enough to react accordingly in terms of turning on or turning off production and transferring fabric and components to more appealing product styles where sales performance and fast emerging trends dictate.

What is key to be a successful buyer is the ability to work as part of the overall team and influence the rest of the team's activities which could be in the form of a managerial and developmental capacity that could also include both their peers and superiors.

The display of emotional maturity and commercial acumen within the controlled parameters as set by the merchandising arm in terms of the budgets, the number of product options and display space constraints is absolutely essential.

The same principle applies to the relationships that need to be maintained with the technical teams in regard to the use of the most appropriate fabrics which meet the product form and function demands in addition to ensuring that the brand standards of the garment are observed.

The fact that potentially the buyer together with the other retail players will be dealing with three to four seasons simultaneously at different stages for each season makes their task even more complicated. To clarify the phenomenon a bit further, the journey of this book attempts to describe the process from beginning to end for one season but while trading in the current season the thoughts and strategies are being developed and documented for two or possibly three seasons ahead followed by the range development leading up to the production taking place for next upcoming season.

The ability to absorb and interpret vast amounts of information from various sources, much of which originates from complex IT systems, can present a challenge to those who are not analytically minded. Systems have altered the scope of the traditional buyer from being a pure "touchy feely art skill" to having to develop basic technical abilities through the continual emergence of innovative systems which have become a great advantage to the role.

Some buyer's, such as those for knitwear, ladies structured underwear, tailoring and footwear will require more expert fabric and garment construction knowledge of their respective industries in comparison to individuals who select the more straightforward cut, make and trim products such as dresses, blouses and casual trousers.

As the trade environment has become more global and through information technology development it is much faster, interactive and has enabled business to be done more effortlessly from a home base interacting with many different countries. A great deal of the job is done amongst many new emerging countries which has led to a need for urgency and nimbleness in order to locate the most effective plants that meet the quality requirements, be able to assess the required technical abilities, understand the economic and cultural demands of the respective countries as well as the logistical peculiarities and government regulations that may exist.

The sourcing of production has to take on different approaches as the pros and cons of dealing internationally needs to be carefully weighed up against those of dealing with the ever diminishing number of local suppliers. A critical factor is that suppliers must be ethical in terms of labour practices, remuneration, waste management, working conditions and safety. If such conditions are not met it is counter to the interests of the retailer to be associated with such suppliers from both a moral point of view and the exposure of malpractices could lead to negative media reports and the retailer will suffer the consequences that accompany such deeds. The measurement of performance is therefore key to gauging the effectiveness of suppliers.

In larger organisations a buyer will probably be supported by an assistant or trainee buyer who will normally be a person who wishes to pursue a career in the field. They will be largely responsible for the organisation of the ranges, perform some clerical work whilst preparing products for garment reviews, monitoring the product development critical path and production milestones, liaising with suppliers and technology as well as deputising for the buyer when they are out of the office.

A point to note is that the relationship between buyers and suppliers often develops into more than a pure business association due to the fact that they spend much time travelling together and working closely with one another building ranges. Close familiar relationships frequently make it difficult to maintain a business like association for the mutual benefit of both parties and can cloud business decision making and judgment. The temptation of bribery and incentives in exchange for placing large orders may be desirous. For newer naïve buyers the rule that the supplier is not your friend should be firmly applied simply because they are more easily seduced by grandiose lunches and gifts as many have unfortunately found out the hard way when they move on and are no longer of great importance to the particular supplier.

A way of balancing the workloads or ranking of buyers and merchandisers is to evaluate the actual number of suppliers, stock keeping units or barcodes being handled by each buyer and then make comparisons regarding workload and productivity of each buyer to established benchmarks.

Merchandisers

The merchandiser or planner applies their focus on maximising profitability from the business end. This is done largely through the analysis of historical sales and the influence of the trend direction to determine the range categories and product breakdown within the overall sales budget.

The role defines what stock levels are required to meet the preset targets such as seasonal stock turnover or forward stock covers based on the sales trends over time. Knowing these requirements, the merchandiser will determine what intake or purchase quantities are needed at any point in time in the season for the total department and each product category.

The level of the budgets will determine the quantity of options in relation to styling, colour palette, size spans, pricing structure and levels of quality per category that will best service the customer for the time that the goods are expected be on offer prior to a new variety of product being introduced in line with the strategic predetermined seasonal themes.

The merchandiser's job has to be to provide guidance to the buyer to procure within the budget parameters. In short it can be described as providing the buyer with a shopping list or range plan that allows them to go out and fill in the blanks on the plan while buying product. This activity requires the careful management of the "open to buy" which can often be a source of tension between the buyer who always tends to want more and the merchandiser who holds the purse strings. A good deal of emotional maturity and teamwork on both sides is therefore critical for a successful partnership.

Sadly the merchandising role is often branded as a dull, boring number crunching task in accordance with mathematical calculations and while it is this, it can be better described as a creative manipulation of numbers. This task is highly rewarding when positive trade results are achieved or alternatively equally as depressing when these do not materialise. The role can be likened to that of a husband who places his entire salary on a dead cert horse at the races which was by no means appreciated by his wife. However when the horse won he was similarly unpopular for not putting more money on the horse!

Like the buying role, the merchandiser deals with different activities simultaneously as part of the team across a number of seasons and therefore requires high levels of multi-tasking and re-prioritising in the forward planning, problem resolution, critical milestone management, analysis and timeous action implementation.

As the actual trade takes place the results need to be carefully analysed and immediate action plans initiated in order to maximise the opportunities and minimise the levels of markdowns that erode the profits. For these reasons they need to be logical, reliable, and consistent in order to take decisions based on fact.

The regular timeous generation of reports detailing sales analysis, stock levels and forward planning needs are distributed to all team members and to senior management. Often numeric information and commercial analysis is demanded on an immediate ad-hoc basis which adds pressure to the job function and can be very disruptive to routines which in such situations requires the merchandiser to adapt quickly and effectively.

The merchandiser plays an integral role during the presentation at product reviews from the numbers perspective which influences the agreed product mix and justification of the levels of sales budgets.

A detailed understanding is necessary of the stores and the customer profile inherent to respective stores that are best met through the attributes of the ranges in terms of styling, colour and size that are put on offer within the store space constraints. The task is best described by the saying "plan each store as if it is your own" which could never be truer.

With sophisticated IT development and the availability of various software packages, some of which may be developed exclusively for the retailer, will provide quick sales analysis, production planning and afford the ability to make sound decisions based on accurate data. This information is especially necessary to give guidance to the allocator or distributor who will be sending the appropriate quantities to satisfy the store's needs as well as give direction as to the level of repeat buys for products that are trading above expectations.

Some organisational structures do differentiate the allocation function between the merchandiser who focuses on the forecasting and production planning and that of the allocator or location planner who will be responsible to distribute the product to the stores in the most appropriate combinations of styles, colour and sizes that meet the store profiles. This function can be housed as an extension within the buying division or may be part of a separate centralised group where an allocator may be responsible for a diverse number of departments. The benefits of such a centralised structure is that there could be a cost saving advantage especially where smaller departments do not warrant a dedicated staff member but added to this is a pool of knowledge which develops a highly skilled team who are able to cross pollinate information, coordinate inter departmental promotions effectively and develop consistent techniques and skills. The identification of common emerging trends will contribute to the optimisation of sales and assist in the control of stock quantities at a very detailed level and thereby maximise profits. Close connections to the departmental merchandisers is maintained to ensure that their actions are aligned to the departmental strategy and plans.

The need for the diversification of the function also makes more sense from the point of view in that where the distribution function is retained within the department it inevitably adds to the increasing workload of the merchandiser. The departmental merchandiser task has more and more been impacted on by the development, the implementation and mastering of complex and sophisticated information systems that analyse sales and stock with added forward planning functionalities.

Many such systems are able to integrate with other supporting IT platforms such as supplier performance, technological measurement, critical path management, ordering, logistical and store systems. The added management of a complex allocation system that is necessary to move the stock to stores is more and more difficult with the result that the incumbent is in danger of being drawn into concentrating on and coping with the intricate detail. As a result, the merchandiser runs the risk of losing sight of the bigger objectives as set out in the strategy and operational plans and the consequent degrading of the inherent merchant intuition becomes very real.

The merchandiser needs to effectively manage and develop the merchandising team which can, not unlike the buying role, consist of an assistant merchandiser or trainee who aspire to be a merchandiser.

The role ensures cohesion of activities that have to be synchronized based on actual sales performance through the formalised interaction with other stakeholders such as the buyers and technologists. This contact is usually in the form of regular, typically weekly, departmental meetings where corrective decisions and plans of action are agreed. Frequent association with the points of sale in stores through written communications and reports as well as formal site visits are critical to keep aligned with the customer's preferences and emerging trends and confirm that the stores are sharing the same vision of the overall strategy.

The need to guide suppliers assertively in terms of prioritisation and the achievement of deadlines is critical to meet the suitable stock requirements at any point in time, particularly in relation to peak seasonal periods or key events. For example, once winter breaks, which it does every year except the exact date is not easy to predict, the objective is to have the right stocks in place such as knitwear, thermal underwear, scarves and the like in sufficient quantities to meet the rush. The usual manner to assist in the anticipation of the weather trend is done through reference to previous years data when the weather changes happened which also help to understand variations in out of ordinary performance at particular times. The challenge is therefore to have the appropriate quantities in the stores at the vital time while the maintenance of the balance of stocks must be adequate to cater for the demand without overstocking the stores ahead of planned stock targets. Events such as Easter, Christmas, Valentine's Day and Mother's day are easier to predict and the right levels of stock can be made more accurately available at the right time.

Where suppliers do not meet the required delivery dates, the merchandiser needs to manage the consequences that have to be applied for the underperformance. This can result in some very sensitive and emotional discussions and the negotiation of penalties typically in the form of discounts, sale or return agreements or even total cancellation which will no doubt impact negatively on both parties.

Technology

Technical Teams consist broadly of the fabric and garment technologists. Fabric technologists are highly trained specialists who focus on typically woven or knitted disciplines. Specialised products such as knitwear, tailoring and footwear require added knowledge of components and specific production machinery.

A major portion of the fabric technologist's task is the development and innovation of new fabrics and the enhancement of existing products. New fibres and blends of fibres such as the blending of natural and synthetic fibres, addition of chemicals to finishing process will possibly lead to new inventions and improvements such as better washability, softer handles, easy care properties like easy to iron, crease resistant finishes, rot resistant applications, seamless or seams that are glued that allow for smoother looks particularly for under garments, the evolvement of elastane products such as lycra which revolutionised active and casual wear and the enhancement of thermal properties of winter undergarments. The success of such developments which add to the profitability as well as the form and function necessitates a close working relationship with suppliers, mills and value adders.

Garment technology have the responsibility to ensure that the make-up of the garment meets the set down criteria and the componentry like buttons, interlinings and threads are of the standard that is functional and are not inferior.

Many factories have developed specified technological capabilities that have been built around the production of a particular category of garments relevant to them which vary from factory to factory or even within the same plant. The garment technologist must understand this implicitly and exploit this knowledge to its fullest.

The relationship with the commercial team is sometimes strained as the ideal level of form and function can be challenged by the need to market the product at the most commercially competitive price.

The objective of the garment technologist is to ensure that quality is not compromised. The tasks essential to achieve this can be varied, for example, the assessment of potential manufacturers and fabric mills to ensure that the established standards are achievable, the specification of raw materials, overseeing sampling stages and ensuring that any delays which may result through the process do not compromise the delivery prerequisites.

In safeguarding that the all quality standards are met particularly through the inspection of garments, inspectors need to possess specific skills. Quality controllers should be ethical, sincere and honest, open mindedly being willing to consider alternatives, be diplomatic and tactful in their dealings with people and are able to actively observe their surroundings as well as perceive and adapt to varying situations.

The technologist has an intimate knowledge of the supplier base through historical awareness as well as from continually researching new and existing suppliers. As the sourcing specialist they have to guide buying teams in the selection of the most appropriate manufacturer for the various types of product. It is also very essential that they are conscious of the fabric prominence for the forthcoming season as dictated by the strategies and budget levels to ensure that there is sufficient capacities at the relevant mills to meet the overall demands without compromising quality.

The task of assessing potentially new suppliers is a role that may be included in the stable of the technical team or it may be hived off to defined sourcing specialists who are knowledgeable team members that recognise the strengths and weaknesses of suppliers and based on this where best to place orders accordingly.

Suppliers are assessed on various criteria such as their management infrastructure, financial stability, specialised equipment availability, fabric specialty, levels of innovation, fashion or basic production orientation, the other retailers they serve, their flexibility of cost negotiability and social responsibility policies. Other external factors that may well influence the selection of suppliers could be those like prevailing exchange rates, remuneration policies and physical locality.

In summary, the significance must be emphasised that the diverse buying teams all have to have a clear informed understanding of each other's roles and priorities and that they are aligned to ensure all their tasks are integrated to achieve the goal of delivering consistent quality products manufactured by appropriately skilled suppliers on time all the time. This is especially imperative in the case of more complex products such as corsetry, tailored garments and knitwear.

The handling, packaging, storage and movement of the product through the supply channels has to be done in such a way that the quality of the product is not allowed to deteriorate in any way whatsoever. As some product is sourced from more distant locations a newer trend is to contract the technical function out to approved independent technical service providers or to trusted garment and fabric suppliers themselves who understand and are committed to the standards required. These service providers are thereby able to approve samples, perform quality control and be responsible for the eventual release of the finished product.

THE SELLING OPTIONS

There are many ways to expose the product to the customer in the hope that they will take a positive decision during the shopping process. More often than not, the nature of the product will influence the type of channel that is selected but whatever format that the retail store takes, it remains very simply a part of the integrated supply chain whereby goods are purchased in large quantities directly from a manufacturer, wholesaler, trading house or agent to be sold on in smaller quantities to the end user.

Retailing can be done in the more traditional fixed locations like stores or markets but in recent years there have been the evolvement of more innovative ways of selling the product, a typical example being "pop up" shops whereby a temporary location is used in a busy environment which is possibly a sports event, trade show or similar location where large volumes of potential customers are present. It is also an easy way of promoting goods or the carrying out of special launches.

In the modern era of technology the internet is probably the fastest growing medium through which to sell product. Online websites now exist for all types of goods and all the major traders as well as dedicated online retailers are spending large amounts of money to set up their sites in such a way that they are very user friendly, faster and most attractive with secure, easy payment methods.

The main objectives of such sites is to enable the offer of products, create a level of trust and inspire the customer to make a purchase. The establishment of trust can be aided by the use of testimonials whereby the experience of past customers affirm the selling proposition.

Door to door deliveries at an additional fee or which alternatively may be absorbed by the retailer are carried out by sophisticated courier services from various highly efficient distribution centres. International purchases in foreign currencies are also relatively easy to do in this way and customers receive the parcels within a reasonable period of time.

Another option is that the retailer may choose to carry out picking of stock from brick and mortar stores which are in close proximity to the online customer but it should be noted that this choice does bring challenges in sustaining consistent full availabilities and maintaining accurate data integrity. Similarly, some retailers offer the facility of "click and collect" whereby the customer places an order on line and at a time convenient to them collects the order from a designated store.

The problem that customers do have is that they are not able to try on the garments so retailers need to devise some convenient special service options such as the provision of critical body measurements to assist in the determination of an appropriate size.

Marketing teams utilise various types of techniques to effectively expose the product in the most attractive way to the market. Traditional channels in the form of print, radio, television, in house magazines, flyers, and point of sale material as well as the use of innovative medium such as permeating fragrances and suitable background music or a store branded radio station all attempt to enhance the shopping experience. The use of posters and bill boards, scratch cards and the like are still very prominent in varying formats, however in increasing magnitudes, the creative use of the electronic channels by way of websites, sms, e-mail and social media such as facebook and twitter are now very evident.

The systematic collection of customer data through the interactive media allows the customer profiles to be analysed and targeted in a more scientific way. Loyalty programmes are very popular and mostly reward the customer either in the form of points which can be cashed in at a later stage for the purchase or provide an immediate discount at the till point. Such programmes are not only extremely effective in significantly improving sales and profits but they also allow the retailer to interpret in detail the buying habits of the customer and consequently thereby are able to better service the consumer needs.

While shopping generally refers to the activity of simply buying a product it has become very much a recreational activity whereby a visit to the shopping mall becomes a wonderful experience which may or may not necessarily result in any purchase being made. Some malls may have added attractions such as theatres, ice skating rinks, stages for entertainment and even larger magnetisms such as aquariums and fun parks while facilities such as gyms are not an uncommon appendage. Restaurant and fast food eateries are an integral part which are often positioned in centrally located food halls where both the major brands and specialised restaurants are represented.

The dominant tenants are the major retailers who are regarded to be the crowd pullers. The main mix comprise of large food chains together with typical mass clothing retailers while other stores such as general chains provide the bulk of hard and specialist goods like electronics, appliances, stationery, furnishings, jewelry, pharmaceuticals and sports shops.

A complex combination of line shops who derive their name due to the fact that they flank the interlinking walkways between the major tenants and tend to be more exclusive in their offerings. The rentals are usually at a much higher rate and the closest adjacency to a major tenant comes at a premium. Line shops will typically include outlets such as hairdressers, opticians, beauticians, boutiques, dedicated outdoor gear retailers, accessory specialists, luggage shops, photographic stores, religious retailers selling inspirational product and even tattoo parlours. Other options include the barrow type outlets selling product such as ties and accessories and specialized delicacies.

What is also evolving to a greater degree is the presence of international chains and brands from all over the world as it has become increasingly easy for stores to open due to improved technologies and exposure both from an IT perspective as well as the use of efficient transport methodologies. It has reached a stage where very few major retailers ignore opportunities to trade internationally especially where domestic markets have become saturated and increasingly competitive. The lure of new emerging markets are great but can be challenging in terms of the differing profiles of customers and culture considerations as well as the unforeseen detection of hidden costs.

Malls are strategically positioned close to residential dense areas and the science of the mix of line shops supported by the major tenants are largely influenced by the demographics of the area that they serve. Such malls may be supported by adjacent discount shopping centres which mostly include many clothing, shoe and factory outlet stores. Factory shops enable manufacturers or traders to market over runs, rejects, problem lines at reduced prices in locations that enjoy lower rentals. Liquor outlets, hardware stores and nurseries are also frequently seen adjacent to the main shopping complex.

A factor that should be addressed in the layout of malls is the ease of shopping and the implementation of plans for the free flow of traffic which does not stress the customers particularly during peak times when the mall corridors are jam packed with people. This state of affairs is leading to an ever increasing trend towards convenience shopping where the establishment of smaller shopping centres on the fringes of suburbs dispenses with the anxiety and lessens the time required to complete the shop.

The mall has largely been the cause of the demise of the "high street" store as is evident by the many major chain stores who have succumbed. The operations have consequently closed or have relocated to the shopping centres outside the city. However, there is still a place in certain instances for these stores to remain as is seen in some cities where there is in fact a reverse trend as there is still a density of office workers as well a growing inclination to live within the city centre which has led to surplus office space being transformed into apartment blocks or new developments being constructed.

Traditional general stores and co-operatives offering a broad range of everything for the community and mom and pop family run shops who purchased from the travelling salesman most commonly found in the rural areas are now very far and few between. Centralized shopping locations with all the relevant chains being represented and the influx of the discount shops specialising in goods from the East, some of which have originated from dubious sources, are now in almost every town. This has sadly relegated these old fashioned stores to no longer being in existence.

Franchise stores offer the opportunity for individual traders to invest in a mass retail group and enjoy the benefit of the support from the chain's branding, quality products and marketing strategies. The advantage for the franchisee is that the expansion and market penetration can be accelerated with external investment and they enjoy a commission for goods sold without the risk of stock holding costs, overheads and staffing expenses. The success of a franchise venture will depend mostly on enough working capital, reliable support from the franchisor and the emotional involvement in the business of the franchisee with suitable staff in the right location at affordable rentals.

In days gone by the goods were stored in walk-in counters often being displayed behind glass and in drawers with sales assistants serving the customer from within the unit as well as manning a till stationed at each counter. While this way of serving customers was very effective from an interaction point of view it soon became unsustainable due to the demands of mass retailing and convenience for the customer.

The newer formats of stores are well lit, uncluttered and appealing to the customer. They house easy to access product which is in sufficient quantities with well demarcated information through attractive signage. Displays whether on shelves, tables or garment rails are well thought out and coordinated in cameo presentations that are lit in such a way that suggest to the customer how the product pieces can be worn together in terms of lifestyle and colouration. Displays are adjacent to complementary customer needs, for example women's skirts will be located close to the blouse displays which will be adjacent to the ladies trousers. The ladies outerwear will most likely be next to the lingerie department which will lead into ladies sleepwear. There can also be a thread of the chosen similar colour themes throughout which are being promoted at that point in time.

Focus cameo displays as created by specialist visual merchandisers are located in highly visible areas such as aisles, window displays or walls which change regularly to convey the message of prevailing stories in order to attract and engage the customer. Seasonal changes, special events, promotional activity and colour themes are typically introduced in this way and thereby sustain the impact of newness, freshness and excitement. The customer not only has a pleasant experience considering the proposition but the potential opportunity of a sale is maximised.

Pay points and change rooms are conveniently placed and the design of these units are such that they lessen the frustration that comes with the inevitable waiting periods.

Personal interaction with the customer by any staff member whether they are the sales assistants or management can never be substituted. Service remains of paramount importance in ensuring that they can illustrate to the customer the ways in which styles and colours of the different components can tastefully be worn together.

The need for refurbishment and revitalisation of stores and displays is an ongoing process, which although being costly, regularly presents the customer with a fresh and exciting environment to enjoy the shopping experience and avoid being faced with stale, run down and drab looking stores that undermine even the most attractive merchandise.

As with the buying teams, the selling teams also consist of a mix of skills that are coordinated in such a way that the customer has a most satisfying shopping experience.

The team is spearheaded by general manager who is the head of the store. This position maybe supported by an assistant officer and they will ensure that the overall co-ordination of all the roles will deliver the most efficient running of the operation. A classic structure that they will manage consists of commercial or departmental managers each of whom will be responsible for a segment of the store.

Their role will focus on ensuring that the displays are constantly fully stocked and that they are optimally positioned and displayed proportionately appropriate to the customer demand. By way of illustration the most popular product will normally be in the front of the racks and displayed at the eye level of the customer. The size of the display will be proportionate to the relative demand, in other words, in the ideal world a product that represents twenty percent of the sales will enjoy twenty percent of the space of the relevant display area. Exceptions to this principle may occur where the product may be bulky and will have to be pallet stacked on the floor. An example of this would be nappies, duvets and cushions.

The challenge is to ensure that there is the optimum number of well trained, knowledgeable and positive staff that can best serve the customers without the overhead costs being put under pressure. The service disposition should apply for the entire shopping experience from the time that the customer is greeted at the front door until the transaction is finalised at the till point and the customer leaves the store with the added objective being that the customer will always look forward to returning to the store. Even where a sale may not transpire the offering of advice or patiently helping consider alternatives is part and parcel of ensuring that the customer will return.

Selling teams are supported by other staff functions such as the human resource officer who will be responsible for the personnel functions as well as the shift scheduling of staff. This task is imperative to ensure optimum staffing which is appropriate for the inconstant number of customers over the various times during the day, week month and year of trade. A flexible, part time work force is required which can be more than two thirds of the total store staff and because some of the hours of work are unsocial such as weekend or after normal hours variable rates of remuneration or extra time off will apply.

TRAINING

One of the common requirements of each role that has been outlined is that in order to achieve the highest degree of proficiency there should be a structured methodology of training which will include on the job training where the incumbent is mentored by a qualified and experienced more senior specialist who in turn has had exposure to effective training methods and performance management techniques. Ideally as the trainee progresses they will take on the responsibility for a small section of their department in order to gain the confidence and skills that will stand them in good stead going forward and also serve as a contingency in the event of the loss of senior personnel.

Coupled to on the job training is the formal classroom style lecturing as is necessary and can be performed by either internal or external tutors who will provide the theory that is matched to that which has been learnt on the job. This is of great importance as it is not uncommon that with on the job training exclusively the poor habits of the trainer are frequently transferred downwards.

Equally important is for new appointees to have an understanding and appreciation of the roles of their counterparts in other areas of the business. In order for this to be achieved they should spend adequate time attached to specialists in other fields. An example would be where a buyer in training would need to spend time in stores interacting with customers, at suppliers, with merchandisers, technologists, the marketing team and packaging specialists, in the warehouse and with the logistical experts including forwarding agents. These attachments should be well thought out with specific objectives in mind and followed up in formal reviews in front of a panel of experts from each area who test their understanding. An independent representative from human resources should also be present to ensure that the consistency of standards applied across the business is maintained and the assessment is objective without any personal bias of trainers subjectively influencing the conclusions either positively or negatively.

Overall, in order to guarantee the creation of professional teams is that the training needs to be consistent and that the outcomes deliver broadly the same standard of qualified appointees. An outstanding illustration of this is where the customer enjoys the same high level of service from sales personnel in whatever store they frequent or suppliers enjoy similar levels of proficiency across different buying teams.

Two common errors that are made which dilute the depth of knowledge is firstly, the situation where managers are appointed over areas where they have had none or very little exposure or experience. This leads to them being unable to assess the information presented with authority and makes the mentoring role required to develop juniors in some cases ineffective.

The second error that is relatively common is the assumption that because the person may be extremely proficient in performing their task it will automatically mean that they will be equally good in being the boss. The truth is that the exact reverse may well apply in that they may not have the inherent management skills and invariably will over focus on the detail and still have the desire to continue doing the work themselves.

Both such scenarios will lead to the situation where the officeholders will lose confidence in themselves and the respect of their subordinates will be weakened.

PROCESS FLOW OF KEY RETAIL ACTIVITIES

While a lot of activities are required from conceptualisation to the eventual offering of a completed product to the customer they do nevertheless follow a relative set sequence of events even though there may be at any point in time where they can possibly overlap each other.

In the sections that follow, the detail required for each key activity will be explored and their relationships and dependencies on each other will be highlighted.

The journey commences broadly with strategy formulation and the strategic planning for each stakeholder area, the creation of a merchandise plan through to the buying of the product within the budgetary parameters. The commercial team have the support of the technology teams to establish the technical requirements as well as the sourcing of appropriate suppliers in order to enable the production of the product.

The packaging is detailed to assist in the marketing of the product and protect the garments in transit and storage. Orders are initiated and the critical production milestones are managed in such a way to ensure delivery deadlines are met timeously.

During production the quality inspection and supplier performance management takes place and once the order is complete the products will be allocated and delivered either directly to stores or to a storage facility. In some instances there may be value added processes applied to the goods after which they will be transported to stores.

Once the goods are on offer to the customer the sales are analysed and reviewed in order to make adjustments where necessary. At the end of the season the lessons learnt are noted and applied to the strategy development for the new season.

STRATEGY

Strategic planning

Leading companies are well aware that to maintain the competitive edge and sustain success they need to have an effective strategic plan in place.

The strategic plan can be likened to a battle plot as it is the preplanned setting of goals which are quantifiable as well as achievable and outline the path of action that all stakeholders need to follow to win the battle. The action is implemented through the use of specific and measurable objectives together with tactics to ensure that the clearly stated mission as to why the company exists is achieved. A point to note is that the more adventurous the strategy the higher is the risk involved but may reap more reward. It is important therefore to reiterate that the mission must be realistic and adaptable.

The strategic plan answers the question why which differs from the business or operational plan which answers the question how. The objectives and tactics required in order to achieve the strategic plan will be reflected in an operational plan.

A standstill assessment of the current status will identify what needs to change and that which is not performing. The purpose will be to establish where the focus should be applied and question if the current incumbents being held responsible are the most suitable and whether or not additional resources are required.

A strategic plan is required to cater for the consistently changing and more complex environments which need to be identified through detailed strengths, weaknesses, opportunities and threats analysis of both internal and external factors. Examples of these may be a stable internal infrastructure, exchange rate fluctuations, new competitor activity, potential new markets and the like. The plan should provide a view of the future so it is clear as to what the business is required to do in order to survive in the new world and best serve the customer in a sustainable manner.

While it is great to have a strategic plan, it is equally important that the plan is regularly reviewed and updated and is relentlessly followed. For this to happen effectively the format has to be efficient, flexible and interactive. As planning is an ongoing process, so the setup must allow for information to be captured, shared and updated in real time which will alert the retailer to the warning signs as to what could happen in particular situations and have alternative ideas in place that can be easily and quickly implemented.

The type of points that need to be addressed in the drafting of a plan is to know what the vision together with the corresponding mission is. The relevant customer and their desires specific to the retailer have to be intimately understood. Competitors should be clearly identified as well as the factors that will influence both the customer and the competitors of the future.

From a broader perspective it is wise to evaluate the forecasts of respected scenario planners and attempt to understand any possible impacts on the business and trading environment that may or may not evolve.

Diagrammatically the process cycle of strategic planning can be depicted as follows

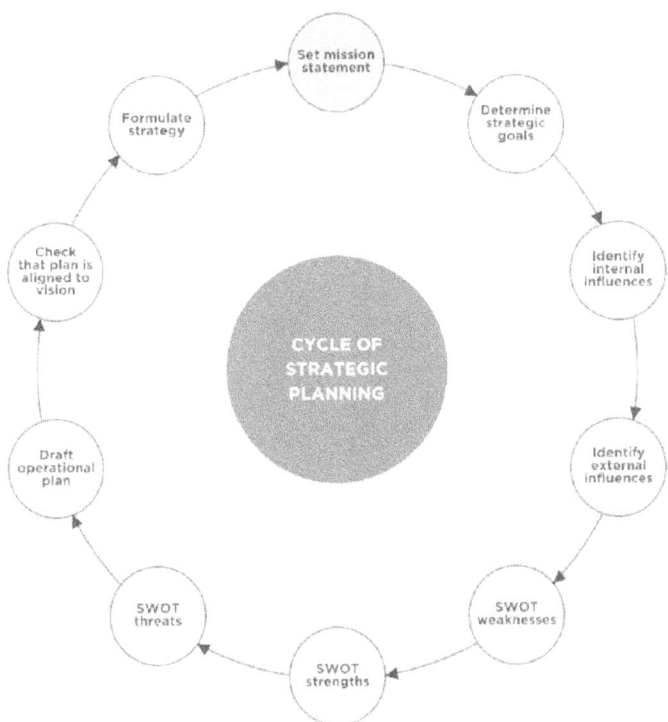

A simplistic example of a strategic plan of a hypothetical retailer can be as outlined below

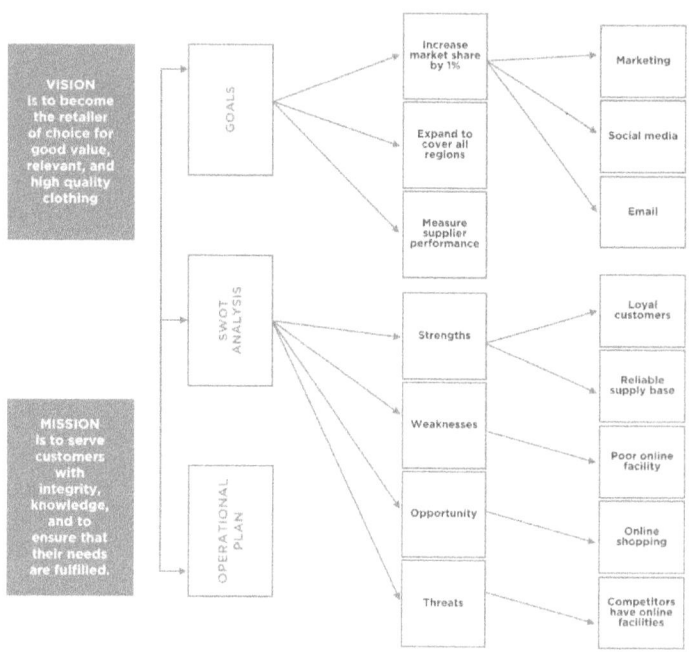

The corresponding operational plan for the strategic plan above will therefore possibly look like

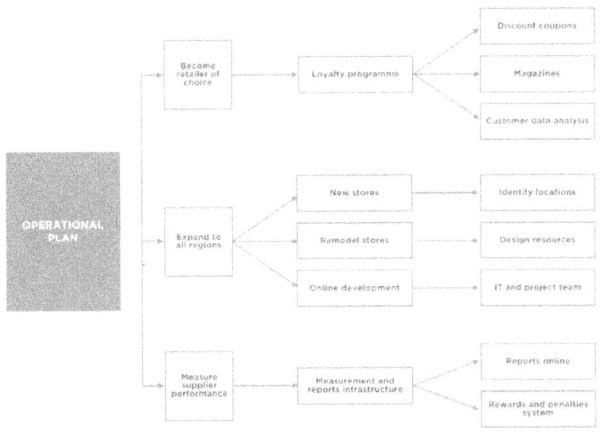

The consequences of poorly thought out strategies can be devastating. There are many examples of once extremely successful chains whose buildings that were landmarks are today parking garages. Retailers who have a tendency to doubt outlooks are often displayed through the rear view mirror images which tells us from where we have come has always worked and the subsequent question asked is more often than not "if it is not broken why change?"

The very successful, intelligent captains of such firms often succumb to the destruction of once successful business for a number of reasons. The fear of change is more often than not the cause because the potential is not viewed as an opportunity but rather seen as a risk. When there is a trend being followed by competitors or new entries to the market an air of arrogance takes hold and the dogged belief is upheld that the current trading philosophies which are set in concrete will withstand the onslaught and any other unfamiliar options are doomed to failure.

Taking the importance of new strategic objectives seriously is seen at times as just another routine task on the calendar which needs to be completed but in reality the focus quickly apathetically returns to complete the current responsibilities as before to sustain the operation.

The lack of the leaders who see the big picture and miss out on the benefits in total can be extremely damaging. In their place is only those who resolutely continue the practice of working within their own relevant areas of control and comfort zones and do not consequently contribute to the achievement of an overall vision. Invariably it is the personal objective that dominates which is one of self-preservation as is reflected in the view that as long as their area has performed within the required parameters any failures that may arise cannot be attributed to them.

Similarly some organisations, characteristically those that are family driven or are by nature very staid with autocratic leadership frequently lack imagination to foresee change or are reluctant to "think out of the box" and consequently there is an unwillingness to innovate. When such an approach is challenged it is often met with obstinacy to hold on to what's more certain, defined and secure which is in the present. The result is that the argument for change is often justified by making it sound less critical than it really is and is stereotypically confirmed by erroneous comparisons to other case studies.

The success of retailers is frequently measured by the scale of operations and share value rather than by the product quality, shopping experience and resultantly the usage of the phrase "customer service" becomes trite and is nothing but just a throw away statement.

In many circumstances operations were dominated by the availability of easy credit at stores where the needs of the customer were broadly projected and the product was bought in high volumes across a limited number of categories to lever better prices from vendors. The driving force was to sell them as quickly as possible using mediocre service. Consequently innovation and revitalised selling formats were almost totally stagnant for many years.

The reality is that the consumer has become conscious to this fact and it does not inspire them any longer to remain loyal to a specific brand but rather to source out the retailers who are sincere in their messages, offer service of difference whereby the customers can truly appreciate a better experience. Much of the success of the newer revolutionary retailers is that they have identities that the consumer associate with which may be cultural such as an eastern philosophies, sporting associations with an emphasis on lifestyle and role models where the markets are not dependent on mass and discount but on meaning and have become communities in themselves.

The point needs to be made that it takes some bold mind shifts when the writing is on the wall that failure is imminent and the need to manage the way out of the situation calls for outside interventions, new strategies and tactics and respect in order to emerge on the other side of the storm successfully.

Strategic stakeholders

In a clothing retail environment the typical individual stakeholder areas need to focus on their independent strategies for a specific period of time that together must be aligned to meet the overall company strategy. It is therefore imperative that the different areas are scrutinized and activities are adapted to ensure that this objective is achieved.

Illustratively the various pertinent strategic focus areas are depicted as follows

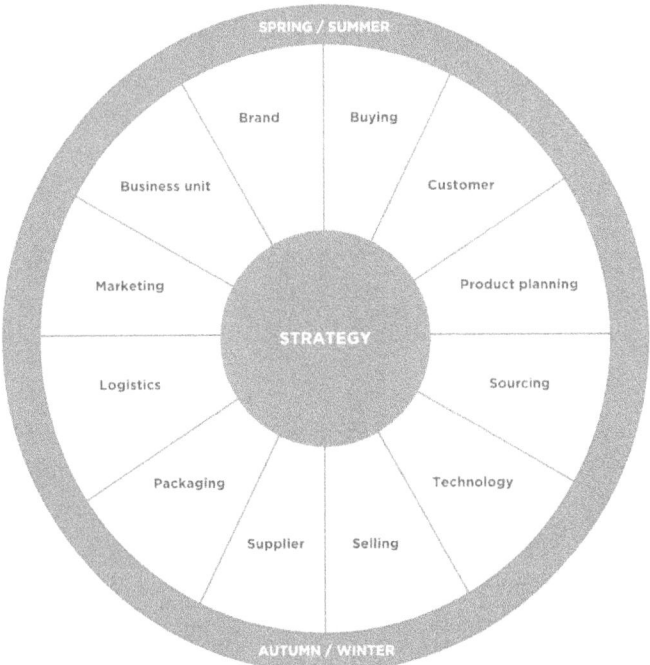

Business unit strategy

The leaders representing each of the key areas will construct the overall company strategy for a specific period as well as for an extended future time thereafter.

Fundamental for the company's success is the need to nurture an environment wherein all employees are able to conduct their business in pleasant conditions with fair remuneration enjoying personal recognition and job security.

Factors which will be taken into account in the construction of the overall strategy will be the historical trading performance, current business trends, competitor activity, customer demographics, the growth of new emerging markets, economic trends like increasing fuel prices and interest rates, and evolving trends which can translate into new business opportunities as is the case of procuring better value goods from off shore suppliers and initiatives like the exponential increase of on line shopping.

Using internal and external research with the evaluation of past performance will determine the budget targets, key performance goals and market penetration potential.

Out of the strategic workshop a corporate operational plan will be developed and disseminated to the relevant business areas to give guidance in the construction of their own individual strategies to ensure that the overall objectives of the company are met. This would include the need for shifts in retail, financial, marketing, information technology, real estate strategies, the sourcing of suppliers, logistical processes and provide individual operational plans that will ensure that the modifications and new initiatives are all catered for. Examples of changes may include action to penetrate new or better serve customer profiles, expand retail channels such as on line, to open new stores in new locations, implement innovative systems and reduce lead times. Fresh initiatives may be in the form of adding new product types, acquisitions, enhancing logistical operations and implement an innovative variation of loyalty programmes.

Brand strategy

A considered view of the external and internal retail landscape has to be documented and understood. In order to enable this, team members in the buying groups, marketing, sourcing, technology, packaging, the store's visual team and designers will workshop the information gathered from past sales performance and take on board lessons learnt from the previous season, market share information, loyalty programme data analysis together with trends evident at global trade shows, catwalks, other retailers, suppliers, internet and social media.

The task that is undertaken is the formulation of the direction of emerging trends in designs, core fabrics, colours, technical innovation and packaging, marketing communication as well as the highlighting of key global customer and lifestyle trends. These developments can be applied to the future season together with the identification of potential customer penetration opportunities which is vital in the input for the construction of the group buying strategies.

Service is very much a critical component of branding particularly where the retailer is own brand active and that if unsatisfactory service persists it will be unlikely that the operational expectations will be delivered.

The positioning of the brand in the market place amongst all other competitors is determined by the attributes that make up the character of the product which helps to evaluate the product positioning in relation to other retailers and assist in ensuring that the right emphasis is achieved in order to maximise opportunities. It is critical that fashion retailers have a clear perception as to where they are positioned otherwise customers will become confused and will drift away to alternative contenders who give a clearer message as to what they stand for through the distinctive branding that identifies them.

The market positioning provides the customer with an awareness of the borders wherein the products fall and decree what they would expect to buy from the retailer. A prime example would be where a high fashion retailer introduces a traditional and conservative range of merchandise which would then send out a message that there is an older profile customer shopping in the store. It is therefore important that when a retailer consciously makes changes whether it be style, price or new ranges to reposition themselves that this intention is clearly communicated through appropriate marketing channels to the customer. Failure to do so effectively could result in them running the risk of significant write downs.

The positioning of the brand in the market is best communicated to the customer by building a marketing mix matrix which will be perceived and understood by the customers and will also facilitate benchmarks as points of reference for themselves to compare with competitors. Distinctive branding is achieved through precise marketing, commendable public relations, a sound corporate identity and consistent messaging and image building through advertising.

In the illustration below the attributes are positioned on the varying extreme scales of fashionability and value in the market and serves as a check for the retailer to ensure that they are best catering for their target customer profile by ticking off the qualities that suitably represent their products.

A brand positioning model in the market can be illustrated as follows

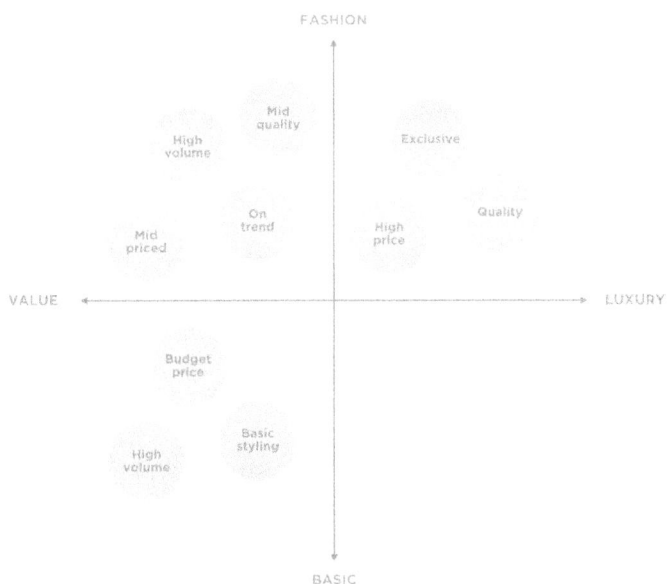

Buying group strategy

Utilising the total company strategy as an input into the buying group strategy for the season will ensure that they stay aligned to the higher level objectives. The similar focus points will be considered and interpreted as they pertain to the specific buying group. Customer and trend direction must be adapted accordingly and the product mix of the group will need to be reviewed as a result.

The trading performance and lessons learnt from the previous season as well as the customer penetration opportunities together with the competitor activity and economic landscape has to be assessed. Adjustments to the targets of the key performance measurements may have to be made to align the strategy.

Retail space requirements needs to be reviewed to accommodate the sales budget changes as well as the product strategy which will include any new initiatives such as special events, promotions and new store expansion.

The strategy has to be tested against the other supporting stakeholders such as logistics, marketing and packaging to ensure that these will accommodate the buying group vision.

Customer strategy

Assuming that your customers are all the same is possibly the biggest error that could be made and the crucial part of growing any business is knowing intimately who your customers actually are.

Understanding the profile and lifestyle of the consumer very well is key to determine that the most appropriate product is developed to cater for the relevant customer segments and to ensure that the product information is effectively communicated through an integrated marketing plan and packaging policy.

Various factors have an influence on the profile of customers and knowledge of these will assist in the categorisation of customers and apply the most fitting methodologies that are a prerequisite to best serve them. Generally the typical segmentation of customers is determined by their behavioural needs, their psychological characteristics and the environment wherein they exist. The strategic objective is to provide the customer with products that have a combination of integrity, quality and service, represent great value and create an enjoyable shopping experience in a pleasant environment that best suits the target market.

The key factors that influence the customer profiles are

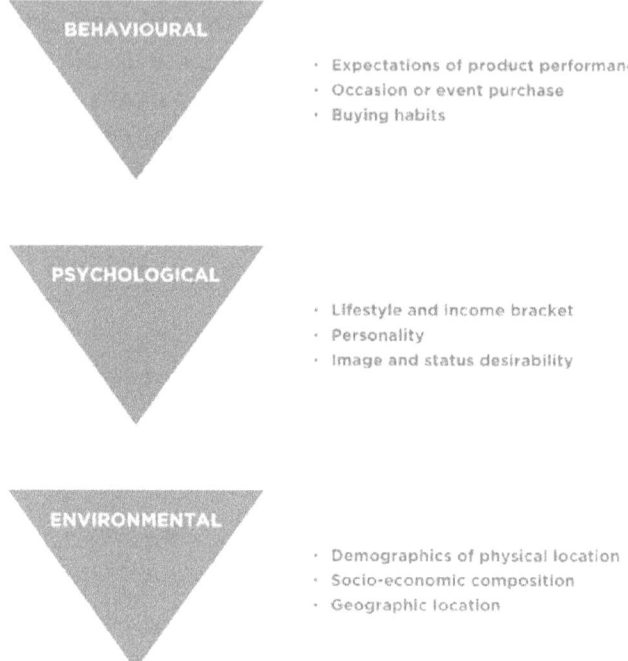

BEHAVIOURAL

· Expectations of product performance
· Occasion or event purchase
· Buying habits

PSYCHOLOGICAL

· Lifestyle and income bracket
· Personality
· Image and status desirability

ENVIRONMENTAL

· Demographics of physical location
· Socio-economic composition
· Geographic location

Behavioural influences are those that in the main are habitual and accommodate the personality traits of the customer. The motivating factor for making a purchase can be varied. A consumer may not be too influenced by the on trend level of the product but will possibly prefer to have an offering that will be durable, practical and functional. If these expectations are not met they will no doubt reject the product whereas at the other end of the scale these factors may be of lesser importance.

The potential customer could be more influenced by that which is socially acceptable and reflected in the media such as magazines, television and exhibited by role models like sports stars, actors and professional people who will play an important part of the selection process. The perception of fashion could differ considerably and therefore the fashion retailer will have to rely more and more heavily on practices that will assist in analysing their particular customer's profiles or that which characterises them more accurately.

Other behaviour traits possibly are where purchases are infrequent and will exist based on a need that a shopping experience will be more of a special assignment to acquire appropriate clothing for special occasions such as returning to work, weddings, holidays or sports events.

Buying habits may include the infrequent visit to stores in order to replace the entire wardrobe on a seasonal basis in order to remain relevant and replace those clothes that have reached their performance expiry date.

The satisfaction of psychological needs such as status and image is a strong motivator in the selection of the styles that will help to achieve this objective. Included will be the perceived expectation that needs to be met by the social circle in which the purchaser moves or reflects a level of wealth that is enjoyed.

There might be the natural drive to exploit the best bargains available and some shoppers may even develop a hobby out of pursuing the greatest values available at a maze of factory and value outlets.

Trawling the glitzy malls and frequenting coffee shops and eateries can be the past time that successfully satisfies the social interaction compulsion.

The more down to earth factors that influence the shopping patterns can be the geographical location where the customer resides. As an example is that a definite difference is detected in style preference between the urbanized to those who live in remoter places where the differing demographics have a probable direct relationship to the social economic environment particularly in terms of gender, occupation, age emphasis, household income and life stage.

With the advance of till technology and the introduction of loyalty programmes it is now possible to gather a wealth of information that describes purchasing behaviour. The information that is harvested is the details of the product purchase such as style, colour, size, fit and price. The frequency and time of purchase and the relationship to other purchases can be analysed as well as the determination of the average spend per customer in different geographical areas is invaluable in building the profile of the customer base. What is of particular importance is the ability to assess the success of promotional launches and the impact they may have on other products during the time of the promotion.

There are some fundamental factors that need to be considered in terms of the population composition which needs to be taken into account in the longer term. A prime example is the greater number of older people who are still economically active at a much riper age. This is evident especially in the case of those individuals who were born at end of World War II when there was a significant baby boom and those babies are now embarking on their so called twilight years. With improved medical technology, healthier eating and lifestyles together with the explosion of health clubs as well as the trend to extend the years of economic activity has had the effect that the twilight years are going to be somewhat longer than in the past.

Another key factor is that the post war boomers enjoyed the availability of easy credit and a large number have accumulated high levels of debt with the result that when they should have been saving for their retirement years and reducing mortgages instead are landed in the situation that retirement is delayed or even worse some will have to continue working until their last.

Forensic auditing studies on mortality rate (SALT Table 1 – 1984-1986} compared in the National English tables for the period 2011 to 2013 showed that the mortality rate improved by 2.5% and 1.9% per annum for men and women respectively. Therefore the assumption can be drawn that a similar improvement going forward is likely to lie at least between these two extremes.

The impact on retailers is the need to make provision to accommodate the active aged in their store design. Store layouts will be required that are easy to shop with minimal confusion, lighting has to be bright and colour corrected to account for failing vision, noise levels need to be reduced to cater for the increased use of hearing aids, product weights must be considered and include an increased carry out service, font sizes need to be larger, shelf heights will have to be such to minimize bending and reaching while packaging should make for easier carrying and opening, queuing philosophies should be reviewed as well as the fitting rooms to permit the comfortable trying on of garments.

At the other end of the scale, the younger generations typically born in the seventies and eighties known as the millennial generation or generation Y are evolving into an extremely different personality to their predecessors and have become legendry in their prolific spending, their brand awareness and because they are technologically advanced this makes them more adventurous. Such characteristics may be in pursuit of their career aspirations as they tend to progress through various places of employment while carving their career at a whim in contrast to their parents who often followed the same occupation for a lifetime. Because these cool, energetic participants are screen junkies they are easily influenced by social media trends and fads. They are therefore able to make informed comparisons and as a result the loyal practice of only shopping at one destination is almost non-existent which places a real test on the retailers to capture a core base market.

Marketing is left with an incredible task to innovate and communicate with this new breed of customer that is arriving on the scene at a rapid pace. Retailers have to start thinking like their customers as in place of window shopping this new breed trawls the internet and stays in contact all the time via the social channels and consequently the retailer need to ramp up their image amongst the channels through financial investment in top class copy writing and superb photographs as well as actively interact on line with their customer. The location of the on line sites should, as with bricks and mortar outlets, be in the best possible space where the greatest exposure to the target customer through the measurement of the number of click troughs is achieved. The offering must be easily found on websites that are advertised forcefully among local advertising vehicles, public relations efforts, promotions and word of mouth.

A popular trend emerging amongst digital enthusiasts is the support for blog sites where the brands are able to speak to an audience in a different light. There is a word of caution in that what they tell the people must be well accepted because should it be met with resistance the consequences could be equally disastrous. Examples exist of some successful fashion blogs that attract thirty thousand hits a day and may have up to two hundred thousand followers on twitter and therefore brands are happy to pay a lot of money to purchase advertising space in these forums. Some brands spend more than fifty percent of their advertising provision on electronic channels and collaborate with bloggers to gain the most editorial exposure. Many designers view the bloggers as their spokespersons as they develop strong relationships with customers by offering fashion tips and advice, the provision of educational material and programmes that help with the customer decision making process as well as at the same time enhancing brand awareness.

Product planning strategy
Once there is a clear understanding of what operational activities are required, the plan of action can be outlined to deliver the strategic objectives and thereby satisfy the goals of the strategy in the most effective way.

What is key in formulating the planning strategy is to set down the clear guidelines in the development of the product mix which will be carefully tailored in the right proportions in order to best serve the customer at the various locations and in terms of styling, colour quantities across the sizes at the most acceptable prices.

For this to be done successfully the overall process of planning follows a set of prescribed activities that make up the mechanics of running the business as well as accommodating the other stakeholder strategies. The steps are a flow of taking in the lessons learnt during the previous season and utilising the learnings as input in the formulation of the strategic goals for the future season.

The goals will give guidance in the preparation of the level of budgets determining the product mix and setting up the range plan from which the orders will be placed. Once production has taken place according to the plan the goods will be allocated to the stores taking into account their specific customer characteristics. Sales will be analysed as they occur and as the performance dictates the forward plans will be reviewed and adjusted appropriately.

Diagrammatically the high level key planning steps can be outlined as follows

Sourcing strategy

Utilising the company, brand and buying group strategy together with the lifestyle and trend directions in conjunction with the research of prevailing market dynamics such as exchange rates, quotas and the local industry, a strategy as how to best source products will be drafted for the forward period which could be extended to cover the next few years.

Supplier's performance and ranking needs to be evaluated, the margin policy and negotiation strategies such as open book costing, tenders or cross costing have to be reviewed to ensure that they are in line with the long term sourcing strategy.

Other processes required are the confirmation of core fabrics as well as the key mills. New potential suppliers, including packaging suppliers and countries have to be researched and identified.

Supplier manuals and starter packs must be updated where necessary including the key performance indicators by which the suppliers are measured and the resultant penalties or incentives have to be confirmed and communicated.

Other outcomes of the strategy will be the vision of the rationalisation or expansion of suppliers, the projected volume growth by supplier in order to dictate to the supply chain what the capacity requirements are for the both long and short term corresponding periods.

Technical strategy

The technical teams need to sanction that the correct fabrics, components, dyestuffs and finishes are used and developed to meet the design and buying strategies and the goods are manufactured to the stated quality standards that are offered within the price structure policy.

As the focus is on the technical aspects of the products a careful balance needs to be established as to what the best match is between that which is technically acceptable compared to the commercial viabilities. In order to achieve the right balance there needs to be mature collaboration between the buying and technical teams.

Innovation and refined development opportunities are identified as part of the technical strategy and the plan of action and accountabilities are stipulated to achieve a competitive advantage and thereby improve market penetration.

Selling strategy

How the product is transferred into the customer's hands is largely dependent on the store format but the manner by which this happens can differ greatly.

In a typical supermarket and mass retail "stack 'em high" environment, transfer takes place whereby the customers serve themselves and payment is made at a checkout. In terms of self-service assistance the only interaction is through the request for help from a roving store staff member or shelf talkers.

The extreme opposite to this is where there is counter service and the customer is served by a dedicated staff member standing behind a unit which is more common in a specialist outlet such as a jewelry store or cosmetic counter.

The approach to the staffing of stores and the change of the roles from real people to technological options are becoming important considerations in the strategic development with regards to selling the product.

A common trend is to house signature ranges within large stores by creating a shop within a shop environment. The examples where this may be a bit indistinct is whereby the product is displayed on self-service shelves but the assistant to customer ratio is very high. An illustration of this is that of dedicated high fashion stores where specialised knowledge is required to assist the customer to make a considered decision. It is therefore absolutely essential to select the most suitable selling strategy option that will optimally serve the customer.

Technology is fast changing the face of servicing the customer much in the same way the introduction of barcodes did in the past. The use of robots to replenish shelves as well as the counting of inventory or retrieval of orders is a reality in the making. Technical packages that measure the customer's preferential purchases and reconcile to previous purchases to feed the data base in order to understand and know the person are now common place. Other applications are such as the body metrics programmes that take body measurements in an instant and recommend the appropriate size of garments. At the checkout the process can be accelerated significantly where the trolley of product can be scanned as an entity without the comparative laborious task of handling, scanning and packing of the individual items. The viability of the investment and the impact on staffing structures in such like developments should be weighed up carefully against the competitiveness and efficiencies that they will deliver.

Supplier strategy

The relationships with suppliers is key to a successful business in order to ensure that the trade is sustainable and fair in the long term. The strategy needs to be formulated in a way that it safeguards the consistent achievement of the key performance targets, where there is regular feedback and a system of incentives and penalties can be applied to maximise the efficiencies. The strategy would stipulate that the relationship that should be strived for is to partner with suppliers who are dependable in terms of meeting delivery deadlines, supply the quantity requirements accurately, are cost efficient, maintain high quality standards, display innovation, have fair remuneration policies and are environmentally sensitive which will all be for the mutual benefit of both parties.

Packaging strategy

The packaged presentation of the product needs to be done in the most pleasing way and must meet the overall design and product standards as set out in the respective guidelines.

Because purchases are emotionally important, clear communication throughout the purchasing process is critical, the message should convey an aesthetic, value for money and ecological consideration that appeals to the customer.

The design of primary packaging must be complimentary in theme across all the different ranges while remaining functional, secure, cost efficient, environmentally friendly and informative.

The strategy for packaging needs to be an all-encompassing one so that there is consistency across the brand values, corporate design and colours of the company. Ideally a standardised process should be in place with clear roles and accountabilities in terms of design, briefing and tracking of development progress as well as for the resolution of issues.

Packaging development and procurement is more often than not quite costly and therefore is frequently a point of tension between the commercial arm and the packaging department in order to keep expense to a minimum. For this reason there is the need for a complete and clear packaging budget policy.

Efficient critical path management of packaging is crucial to ensure that the deadlines in terms of concept approval, design, printing, manufacturing, technological approval and final delivery are aligned to meet the product critical dates and thereby ensure that deliveries are not compromised.

Secondary packaging in the form of transit cartons or hanging formats need to be protective in order to preserve the quality specifications and make sure that the presentation standards are well maintained. The form and function of the product has to be safeguarded in a cost effective way while conforming to all legal requirements.

Logistical strategy

The logistical approach to best serve the stores requires options which effectively deliver the goods to the customer from diverse sources at cost efficient rates, as quickly as possible, while maintaining the integrity and quality of the goods.

For the movement of product from a supplier through an arrangement of regional warehouses enables deliveries to be closer to the retailer's outlets. This may take on the method whereby the supplier delivers to a number of regional warehouses throughout the country, which receives and stores the goods awaiting allocation instructions from the commercial office that trigger a pick and pack operation prior to distribution to the stores in the respective area.

Storage and the distribution operations in a central warehouse are normally situated in the major centres where the acceptance of the delivery takes place from suppliers who are in the closest proximity. Once the allocation instructions are received the product is picked and packed prior to distribution to local stores. For those stores that do not fall in the service area of the receiving warehouse the goods are trunked in bulk to other geographical locations where the pick and pack function will be actioned and thereby ultimately all the stores throughout the country are catered for.

Much of the volume of stock held in the warehouse is received ahead of the season and the frequency of deliveries may well depend on factors such as minimum order quantities, pack sizes, proximity of suppliers, particularly in the case of off shore manufacturers.

Distribution models also exist where there is a flow through consolidation at distribution centres and the physical storage of the product is pushed back up the supply chain to the manufacturer. Allocation instructions are communicated to the supplier to enable the product to be picked, packed and labelled at individual store level which is then delivered to a distribution centre. Consolidation of the cartons from all suppliers takes place at store level to await dispatch. The advantage of this format is that the handling of product is minimised and the cost of storage for the retailer is reduced.

Movement of overseas manufactured goods is done in the main through freight and forwarding agents who manage off shore consolidation points. Suppliers deliver containers or part deliveries to these facilities and the agent will implement the logistical arrangements for the merging of the goods for retailers prior to dispatch via sea or air. In some instances the goods may be picked, packed and labeled at this facility ready for distribution to stores upon arrival as is done with local suppliers. However, this is really only practical for once off or initial deliveries and does not suit follow up or continuity replenishment orders.

Critical to the efficient movement of product will be that of ensuring the correct documentation and tariffs are all in place in order to facilitate the free flow of product through customs and excise. Once the goods arrive in the destination country they are cleared and delivered to the retailer. Thereafter the same process is followed as for the local suppliers and in all likelihood utilises the model where goods are delivered to a central warehouse which will be in the city of the port where the goods have been offloaded.

Marketing strategy

Marketing teams use various types of promotional strategies to effectively expose the product in the most attractive way to the customer. Traditional mechanisms in the form of print, radio, television, in house magazines, local media, flyers, shelf talkers, posters, bill boards, scratch cards and the like are still very prominent.

However in growing magnitudes is the creative use of the electronic channels such as internet, sms, e-mail and social media like face book and twitter.

Together with the increased usage of technology a clear distinction has developed between the brand building objective and that of the management of the retailer's reputation. Some of the larger retailers have put specific management structures in place to perform this task. A reservoir of goodwill needs to grow in order to enhance the reputation in the eyes of the consumer. In the same way that positive comments grow the reputation, negative comments may potentially be as destructive when issues arise but in such cases where the reputation quotient is high there is evidence that the level of criticism is less severe.

The focal points of reputation measurements are how much the retailer stacks up in terms of trust, esteem and admiration for the way they operate in the field of not only the product performance and innovation but also that of their workplace environment, the decent governance they uphold and the moral citizenship they display within the community.

Loyalty programmes are very popular in rewarding the customer either in the form of points, coupons or discounts. Such programmes are not only extremely effective in significantly improving sales and profits but they also permit the retailer to analyse the buying habits of the customer in detail and consequently are able to better service the consumer needs. Programmes also enable the retailer to build a data base through which they can communicate directly with the customer in terms of highlighting special offers, the awarding of gift vouchers for special events such as birthdays through using various mediums such as newsletters, e-mail, social media and the postal service. Examples of such programmes are not only to reward for purchases above a certain amount but may also be for first time buyers, freebies such as buy one get one free while some are targeted at specific categories of product and account holders. The objective of a good loyalty programme strategy should be to attract and keep new relationships, embed positive perceptions of existing customers, heighten brand awareness and not necessarily simply just provide a service for those discount hungry customers who see such incentives as a means to save money.

Social responsibility is incorporated in the marketing strategy in that it displays the commitment to the community, the disadvantaged and the development and welfare of employees in the form of initiatives other than just those which are purely profit motivated.

BUYING GROUP ORGANISATION

A characteristic merchandise hierarchical organisational structure of a retailer is illustrated below where mainstream buying and merchandising function cascades down from the highest platform to the lower department level details. Service areas as depicted on the right hand side of the diagram support the core functions.

Typical buying group organisation chart

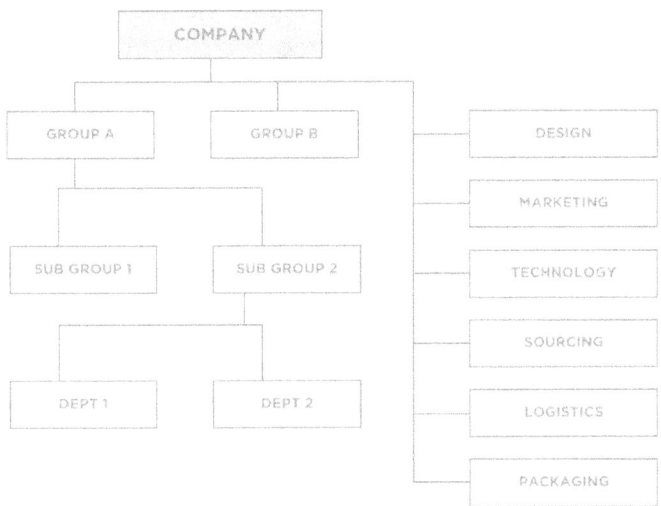

The basic hierarchical staffing roles of all the key players in a mainstream buying structure is outlined diagrammatically below.

The chief executive officer is clearly the leader together with the board of directors who ensure that the overall company strategic intent is delivered and the profits are achieved as reward to the shareholders to whom they are accountable.

Group executives look after the broad category types such as menswear, ladieswear and childrenswear. The responsibility is to ensure that the group delivers to the set strategy and is reacting properly to changing trading conditions while still meeting the profit objective.

Within the mainstream groups such as menswear a sub division into sub groups may well take place probably by lifestyle such as formal wear and casual wear. The category manager is responsible for the mini business or sub group with set turnover targets, profit objectives and strategies.

Buyers, merchandisers and location planners operate at the departmental level down to the lowest degree of product being colour and size and are responsible that the management of the detail delivers the eventual goals at all the higher levels.

Key staffing hierarchy posts of a buying organisation

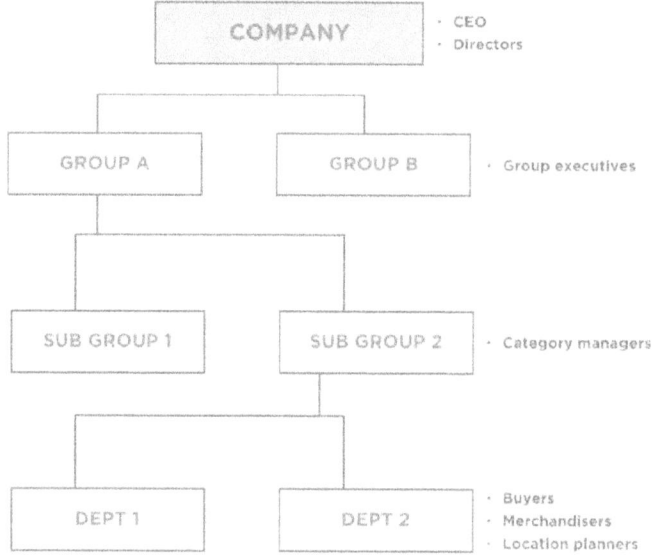

MERCHANDISE PLANNING

The main purpose of merchandise planning is to forecast sales for the period under review and manage the levels of stock in the correct assortments based on the historical performance and forward trends. Buyers are guided to procure within the parameters of the budget and ensure that the right product is delivered to the right stores in the right quantities of style, colours and size in order to maximise the sales and profit objectives and minimise mark downs. In order that this is done effectively it is important that the numerical planning is done accurately and is able to be measured in line with a set of predetermined criteria.

It is a known fact that things do not always go according to plan so it is equally important to measure the actual performance against what was originally envisaged and recommend corrective action where deviations occur. This may take various forms whether it is buying more of a style if possible, turning off supply or converting styles into those that are more in demand. Allocation quantities need to be reviewed in line with the individual store performances. These actions need to be done as urgently as possible after the analysis is completed.

Key performance indicators

For stakeholders to be able to check whether the performance is on track to achieve the strategic objectives it is measured against a suite of pre-set performance indicators. The most common performance pointers which are assigned targets that will deliver the desired finanancial reqirements, are the following.

Sales
Markdowns
Buying margin
Sales margin
Stock forward cover

Stock annual turn

Return on inventory investment

It is absolutely imperitive that these indicators are clearly understood by all members of the retail team both in the head office and stores and what role they play in the support of them.The measures are almost always referred to in financial reports as share holders utilise these to determine their level of confidence in the company performance.

 A brief explanation of each one of these as well as how they are derived is as follows.

Sales are recorded and planned in monetary value although reference is frequently made to volumes in order to plan production capacity requirements. The monetry value measurement is expressed as a percentage in relation to another value which is normally against the comparable sales of the previous year or against the budgeted sales for the correponding current period. The measurement within the stores can also be done such as the takings per square metre to assist in the apportionment of amount of display space deserved by product categories within the departments . Sales per square metre also serve as a benchmark target to which minimum performance is required to asses the viability of carrying particular ranges and is a good measure which can be referenced by the buying teams when probing the sales performance of product in stores. It should be understood that various designs of display equipment such as wall displays, racks and tables are also apportioned varying relative square metreage rates.

The same principle can be applied to dividing the expenses into the amount of saleable square metreage and therefore the profit per square metre can also be determined. Similarly sales per hour and average sales per customer are helpful in terms of staff scheduling and employing staff in functions that are balanced to return an acceptable rate of sale per employee.

Growth percentages compared to other periods can identify problems or successes in buying, product flow, inventory levels, merchandising, advertising assesment thereby can be better understood where these are distorted due to changes in the environment such as selling space expansion or store closures, competitive activity or out of the ordinary events.

The calculation of the growth percentage is the difference between this year and last year sales divided by the total sales for the same period.

Assume last year sales was 700 and this year sales are 900. The sales growth would therefore be [(900-700)/900] x 100=22.2%

The desired sales level can also be derived by applying a percentage increase.

Assume a percentage increase of 10% is required against last year and the sales for last year is 700. The required sales budget for this year will therefore be 700 x 1.10=770

It should be noted that in terms of percentage growth a differentiation should be made between overall growth where the total increase of the department includes all products in contrast to a like for like increase which is between identical products from the corresponding season in the previous year and represents the true inflationary measurement.

The common opinion is that the achievement of this measure is the crucial to ensure the delivery of the other key indicators.

Markdowns are inevitable in some form or other. The requirement to reduce merchandise can be due to various reasons such as sales being below expectation, the need to clear stock due to necessity and allowing the management of the pipeline to facilitate newness to flow through and also to be able to contain stocks within the parameters of the set stock targets. Markdowns need to be provided for by way of a budget in spite of it being difficult to predict the exact nature of the markdown at the lower levels of product.

The markdown value is the monetry value by which the product was reduced.

Markdowns are measured in percentage terms derived by the relationship of the markdown value to the total retail sales for the period.

Assume for the period the value of markdown was 1000 and the corresponding sales were 10000. The markdown percentage would therefore be

(1000/10000)x100=10%

The size of the provision for markdown is dependent on historical data and the acceptable percentage in relation to the original sales budget or retail selling price. The levels of markdown will vary dependent on the nature of the product.

Typically the more high fashion type product such as ladies tops will have a higher markdown percentage to sales which can be as high as fifteen percent while the very basic product that is sold as a continuity item rather than a single input such as underwear will be much lower and may even only be done routinely to flush older merchandise out of the system. In order to cater for these variances the buying margin policy for the various categories will accordingly reflect these levels of risk.

Product is generally marked down on the go or alternatively the affected goods are removed from display until a planned seasonal sale which may be two or three times per annum. The main reason for higher levels of markdown is most often that the customer rejects the offer through disillusionment or when the most popular colour or size is not available. Fragmentation of ranges inevitably slows the rate of sale and consequently results in displays becoming untidy and disorganised as well as restricting the display space required for new lines. Space constraints often lead to the product being removed from display never to see the light of day again until the major seasonal sale.

Depending on the overall demand for fragmented pockets of stock it may be considered to recall all the odds back to a facility where the goods can be consolidated. New sets of availability are then reported and the goods are redistributed to a limited catalogue of stores that have previously sold the goods at an acceptable level. The risk of this practice is the additional costs which are incurred in handling, transport, repacking, reallocation and redistribution while the goods are still relevant must be such that a profit benefit is still returned. Invariably it is seldom the option that will be selected.

It is not uncommon to pack away seasonal product such as thermal underwear. winter hosiery, swimwear at the end of the season and bring them back to the display units from storage at the commencement of the next season. The shortcoming is that the stock that is re-introduced is often tatty, discoloured and may even be shop soiled and lacking the crispness of fresh goods. If this practice is done it is adviseable to return them to a value add facility where they can be repackaged and correctly price marked for the new season before re-introducing the goods back into the system.

There are various options as how to to deal with reductions. The most commonly used one is that where the goods are marked down on a continual basis as the season progresses. This has the downside that it causes a distraction from new ranges and themes as well as can damage the brand integrity in the eye of the customer. The consumers also tend to adjust their buying patterns in the knowledge that the goods will inevitebly be cleared at a lower price at sometime in the near future and will wait for these occurrences to happen rather than pay the full price. The alternative possibility is to withdraw the affected goods from display until the next specific seasonal sale.

Some chains may have designated stores where sale and distressed goods are combined and sold at reduced prices. Another route that may be followed is to off load the merchandise to jobbers or resellers   at very low prices but in both cases this requires added handling as well as the removal of labelling whilst incurring associated costs.

Buying margin is the margin at which the goods were purchased and is often referred to as the primary margin. This margin is expressed as a percentage and equates to the selling value less the cost value expressed as a percentage of the selling value.

Assume that sales budget for the period is 350 000 and the cost value of the goods purchased is 160 000.

The buying margin is therefore 350000–160000=190000

The buying margin percentage equates to [(350000-160000)/350000]x100=54.3%

The margin is a part of the strategic plan and while there is an overall target for the company, the margins at the the lower levels will vary and will be largely dependent on the fashionability and volume factor of the product. It may also be strategically different in the sense that a product may be sold at a low or even no margin to gain a competitive advantage and thereby increase market share.   As the achievement of the buying or intake margin is critical to the negotiation process it is absolutely essential that it is closely monitored during the procurement process to ensure that the achievement of the overall target margin remains on track.

Sales margin in monetry value is the difference between the actual sales value which is registered at the till and the total cost of the goods sold. The margin is expressed as a percentage and refers to the relationship between sales and cost value and the total sales expressed as a percentage.

Assume that the sales for the period are 200 000 and the cost of the goods sold (including added costs to the base cost of the garment) are 130 000.

The Sales Margin will therefore be 200000–130000=70000

The Sales Margin % will be (70000/200000)X100=35%

The variance of the anticipated sales volumes that were used to determine the buying margin may well be very different to volume proportions that are actually sold and therefore will ultimately deliver a different aggregated sales margin.

The sales margin target is determined by the intake margin after taking expected markdowns into account and has the same logical relationship between the sales value and cost value expressed as a percentage. The difference however is that the actual sales value which is achieved can be very different. It is therefore key to carefully observe what was expected to happen to what actually happened and make sure that is kept in mind when determining forward predictions.

Stock forward cover is the amount of stock required at any one point in time that will permit the forward sales budgets to be achieved. The measurement is usually in weeks and can be expressed as the amount of weeks that is based on the sales plan over the time that it will take for the stock to be exausted.

Stock levels will essentially be higher or lower over time depending on seasonal trends, promotional launches, markdown activities and holiday events. The fluctuations will be reflected in the sales plans and as a result the inventory level will fall and rise in empathy to the sales plan. The target number of weeks can remain reasonably consistent throughout the year and will really only need to be adjusted where situations deem it neccesary such as for factory closures over holiday periods and in the event of build up for new initiative launches such as store openings.

The appropriate number of weeks selected will be determined based on historical data, the strategy intents and the nature of the product. Properties such as fashionabiliy, amount of sizes, lead times from supplier for replenishment, the number of deliveries and turnover of individual stores will have an influence over the number of weeks cover chosen. Commonly the more fashionable the merchandise is, the lesser the number of weeks will be required as the time it is on offer may well be shorter before the next input of new replacement styles in comparison to the basic continuity commodities.

Larger outlets stock tend to sell out at a quicker rate and have greater volumes of sales and therefore are able to survive on less weeks cover compared to the the smaller stores with smaller turnovers which demand a less frequent replenishent and consequently require more weeks cover in order that full availability of all colours and sizes are on offer at any one point in time.

The proximity of stores to the replenishment centres will also have an influence on the stockholding requirements and invariably the rural stores far from the the distribution points may receive less frequent deliveries which take longer to reach them and subsequently these stores will have to have more weeks cover than their relations in the city centres who are closer to the distribution centres.

The principle, however, remains to keep the forward cover as low as possible in order that the stock will be replaced more regularly and thereby is able to generate profit more frequently.

Assume at a point in time the stock holding is 900

The forward sales per weeks going forward are 150,200,130,100,120,110,90,110,140, and so on...

The number of weeks that the 900 worth of stock will last before running out will be

900= 150+200+130+100+120+110+90

This will therefore represent 7 weeks forward cover of stock required to achieve targeted sales.

Stock annual turn is the number of times the stock inventory is sold and replaced in the year.

Each time this happens, profit is generated and therefore the more times this occurs the more times a profit is delivered.

Stock annual turn is usually expressed as the cumulative sales for the previous fifty two weeks divided by the average stock holding for the same period.

Assuming the cumulative sales for the preceding 52 weeks (annual) is 60 000 and the average stock for the period is 15 000 then the stock turn will be 60000/15000 = 4 times.

There is a direct link to stock forward cover value as the lower the number of weeks are, the less the average stock holding will be and as a result the higher the stock turn will be. A point to note about the relationship is that the forward cover can be determined from the stock turn value or vise versa.

The forward cover can be determined from the stock turn value by dividing the forward cover number of weeks into 52 weeks.

If stock turn is 6 then forward cover will be 52/6 = 8.7 weeks

Conversely, if forward cover is 9 weeks then stock turn will be 52/9 = 5.8 times

The significance of the non achievement of the target stock turn can result in the accumulation of higher seasonal stocks which will inevitably be destined for the reduction counters as it will no longer be seasonally relevant and will probably look fatigued and fragmented. The intake of the new seasonal ranges will also be choked in order to remain within the stock parameters.

Return on inventory investment (ROII) Is the measure of the amount of return that is received for the investment in stock.

The profit productivity of the stock depends on the number of times the inventory is sold and replaced and the more frequent these spells are the more times it will generate a profit. The relationship of the cumulative monetry   sales margin value for the period being measured to the average cost value of stock will deliver the number of times profit was made.

The average cost of the stock is determined by the opening stock at the beginning of the period being measured and is added to the stock values per month which is divided by the number of months.

Accept the period being measured is six months and the total sales margin value is 3000. The opening cost value stock of 1000 added to the stock holdings of each of the six months and divided by the number of months plus 1. This value divided into the total sales margin will deliver the number of times profit was generated.

Average   cost   of   stock   =   1000   + (900+800+1100+1200+1000+900)=6900/7=985.7

ROII will be 3000/985.7=3.0

Interdependency of performance indicators
The importance of recognising the interdependence of the performance indicators is paramount.

Should the sales target be under achieved, in all probability the margin targets will not have sufficient sales value to be realised, the stock cover will be higher due to the unsold stock and therefore the stock turn will decrease as will the return on inventory investment.

If the markdowns are higher than originally planned, the margin targets and return on inventory investment will consequently be under achieved.

When the stock sells in different proportions to what was expected and where the products have differential margins, the overall aggregated margin could well deliver a different result to what was anticipated. For example, this phenomenon will occur if sales of loss leading low margin goods exceed budgets and perhaps the higher fashion high margin products sell less than hoped for.

The non-achievement of stock forward cover targets means that the stock annual turns will not be attained and consequently the sales and markdown expectations may or may not be accomplished depending on the severity of the deviation but undoubtedly there will certainly be a resultant impact on the return of inventory investment.

The return on inventory investment will not be realised if any one of the other targets are not achieved.

Profit

The success of any business is measured by the value of the profit it delivers. In order that this is reached it should be well understood as to what profit is and in what forms it is expressed.

Gross profit is defined as the amount which is available after the direct costs of product at the point of sale are deducted from the value for which they are sold. The outlays comprise of the cost of the product, warehousing, royalties, packaging origination and samples.

Net profit is the amount left over after the gross profit is reduced by the non-direct product overhead costs such as rent, salaries, transport, packing materials, as well as the unpredictable costs like markdowns, quality returns, spoilage and unforeseen costs like unplanned airfreighting. Revenues in the form of volume incentives and settlement discounts from suppliers will in turn improve the net profit.

The characteristics of products, for example, fashionability, fragility, proneness to wastage or experience a higher tendency of customer returns will make the product be susceptible to greater values of markdowns. The margins of these products need to take this into account by being set at an above average level.

Profit before tax is the profit after the expenses of the business that are not directly linked to the product such as salaries, store costs, cost of support areas like information technology and marketing are apportioned in some way or other to the product, possibly through the use of turnover contributions.

By means of a matrix the interdependence of the performance indicators may be shown as follows

Note that if the individual performance indicators in the left hand column are not achieved the crosses in the row to the corresponding performance indicators under the relevant headings will also be negatively impacted.

	SALES	MARKDOWNS	BUYING MARGIN	SALES MARGIN	STOCK FORWARD COVER	STOCK ANNUAL TURN	ROII
SALES	X		X	X	X	X	X
MARKDOWNS		X	X	X			X
BUYING MARGIN			X	X			X
SALES MARGIN			X	X			X
STOCK FORWARD COVER	X		X	X	X	X	X
STOCK ANNUAL TURN	X		X	X	X	X	X
ROII	X		X	X	X	X	X

Merchandise planning process

In conjunction with the buyers, designers, sourcing specialists and the technologists, the merchandise planner is responsible for the delivery of the departmental strategy to make sure it is aligned to the strategic intent of the company and the group.

The sales estimation and the planning of the stock levels are done to achieve the sales and margin objectives from departmental level down to the individual product level. Together with the buyer the range planning and building will take place to construct a complete balanced offer of product that satisfies the needs of the target customers.

The intake and orders are carefully controlled to meet the stock requirements as per the plan at any given time while the allocation and distribution of stock is managed in such a way in order to optimise the fulfilment of the customer demands within the selling space available.

The foundation of planning is the manipulation of the components of what is known as the retail balance set which are key to driving out profit.

The balance set components comprise of

- Sales
- Markdowns
- Intake
- Stock

The inter relationship between the balance set components of them can be illustrated as follows

The fundamental calculation rules of the relative components

The common deduction is the necessity to determine how much stock must be bought to meet the planned sales and stock targets or alternatively to consider what the resultant stock levels would be if a pre-determined amount was procured. However the second option is less utilised as invariably the result will be different to that of the original plan.

Assume the components values for a period are

Sales = 1000

Markdowns = 40

Intake = 1240

Closing Stock = 2000

Opening Stock = 1800

Intake = Closing stock plus sales and markdown less opening stock

(2000+1000+40)-1800 = 1240

Closing Stock = Opening Stock less Sales and Markdowns plus Intake

(1800-1000-40)+1240 = 2000

Basic steps of planning process

The principles of planning outlined below is affectionately referred to by some retailers as WISSI which stands for the weekly sales, stock and intake plan. This process has been adopted in some format or other by many merchants worldwide and forms the basis of the logic in technical planning packages which are marketed by a number of software developers. The basic principles are also key to the integration of the planning function with suites of other operational packages such as allocation systems, buying range planning, critical path management, warehousing and distribution applications.

The sequence of steps to determine an intake plan is portrayed as follows

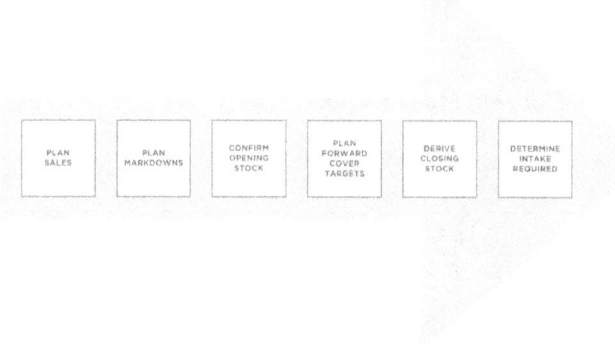

Plan sales involves the forecasting of sales across time, usually for a six monthly season by month by week in a shape that resembles past history and accounts for any strategic intent such as new product launches, store openings, competitive activity and special events like significant world sports happenings and environmental initiatives. It needs to be recognised that some occasions take place at different times from year to year such as Easter and Eid and should be provided for accordingly.

Statistical methods of sales forecasting commonly use the exponential smoothing of trends or weighted moving average options in simple models which are relatively easy to use. For more complex scenarios such as with the introduction of new categories or catering for products with erratic sales it is likely that the predictions will include a safety stock factor to cater for the unexpected. In such cases some companies utilise experts or rely on advanced software to assist in the analysis and formulation of expected patterns

Plan markdowns is required as it is inevitable that not all goods will sell as expected which means that the clearance of oddments is necessary in order to facilitate the flow of newness and other promotional activities as well as relieve any space constraints.

The level of provision for markdowns that is set is influenced by historical trends and the characteristics of the product. The higher the fashionability of the category, the higher is the risk and therefore for such products a higher markdown allowance is necessary. The converse applies for basic continuity product. While it is usually quite easy to accurately predict the amount of acceptable markdown at the higher departmental level, the markdown value contribution of individual line products can differ considerably to expectations.

Traditional types of markdown are the typical end of season cleanouts where there is an aggressive campaign to remove the unwanted product to provide for the introduction of a new seasons launch or for a promotional product sale as part of a strategic intent.

The sell through plan of the sale depends on the intended time the affected goods are placed on offer with scheduled phases of further intermittent reductions and a final liquidation at the end of the period.

Illustratively the markdown activity with probable examples of periods and percentage cuts can be represented as follows.

The progressive phases of markdown sales

Planned promotions should always have a structured post mortem assessment. The framework of the analysis could possibly be done by measuring by how much sales improve for a set period after the promotional launch compared to the level of sales prior to the campaign.

A selection of similar products can be earmarked as control items to which an evaluation can be made in terms of the uplift in sales experienced versus the sales of the control items as well as what the effect of possible substitution purchases were during the same period. Based on these findings the conclusion may be drawn as to the success and viability in terms of increase in profit and market penetration.

Consideration should be given to the space constraints in tight metreage stores to accommodate aggressive promotions. If the volumes and number of customer choices are too great it may result in the operational efficiencies of the store being compromised and will result in the layout to become disconnected from the strategic intent. In these instances it may be considered to transfer some or all of the reduced stock to larger stores.

Confirm opening stock. The starting point for stock represents the actual value of closing stock in the previous period. This has to be recognised as the value affects the required intake particularly in the early part of the new season and may well also have an impact on the level of planned markdown that subsequently may need to be reviewed.

Plan forward cover targets based on the acceptable number of weeks that are strategically agreed for the various categories of products which aid the achievement of the approved stock turn.

Derive closing stock values using the number of weeks forward cover at the end of each month and apply them to the weekly sales plan going forward.

Determine the intake required through the balanced set calculation of closing stock plus sales and markdown less opening stock for each month and the total season.

It should be noted that the weekly sales into the early part of the next season should be taken into account in order to calculate the closing stock targets to meet the forward cover requirements.

In the construction of the simplified model of the intake plan below a flat forward cover of six weeks has been selected for ease of illustration. In reality it may change in the event of special happenings such as factory closures over holiday periods when the routine distribution is disrupted or there is stock build up requirement for new initiative launches, packaging change overs, catalogue adjustments and new store openings.

A representative example of the intake plan

	TOTAL SEASON	MONTH 1				MONTH 2				MONTH 3				
		WK 1	WK 2	WK 3	WK 4	WK 5	WK 6	WK 7	WK 8	WK 9	WK 10	WK 11	WK 12	WK 13
OPEN STOCK	77 000	77 000	79 000	82 000	81 000	81 000	88 000	96 000	98 000	98 000	99 000	98 000	91 000	83 000
SALES	370 000	10 000	12 000	14 000	14 000	12 000	13 000	14 000	15 000	13 000	14 000	19 000	21 000	16 000
MARKDOWN	700				700									
INTAKE	376 700	12 000	15 000	13 000	14 700	19 000	21 000	16 000	15 000	14 000	13 000	12 000	13 000	15 000
FWD COVER		6	6	6	6	6	6	6	6	6	6	6	6	6
CLOSING STOCK	83 000	79 000	82 000	81 000	80 000	88 000	96 000	98 000	98 000	99 000	98 000	91 000	83 000	82 000

	TOTAL SEASON	MONTH 4				MONTH 5				MONTH 6				
		WK 14	WK 15	WK 16	WK 17	WK 18	WK 19	WK 20	WK 21	WK 22	WK 23	WK 24	WK 25	WK 26
OPEN STOCK	77 000	82 000	83 000	84 000	85 000	86 000	87 000	87 000	85 000	83 000	83 000	85 000	85 000	83 000
SALES	370 000	15 000	14 000	13 000	12 000	13 000	15 000	15 000	15 000	14 000	13 000	14 000	15 000	14 000
MARKDOWN	700													
INTAKE	376 700	16 000	15 000	14 000	13 000	14 000	15 000	14 000	13 000	14 000	15 000	14 000	13 000	14 000
FWD COVER		6	6	6	6	6	6	6	6	6	6	6	6	6
CLOSING STOCK	83 000	83 000	84 000	85 000	86 000	87 000	87 000	85 000	83 000	83 000	85 000	85 000	83 000	83 000

Monthly financial planning

As part of the preparation of the intake plan it is good practice to present a basic month by month financial plan for the department. This will enable all the department month by month plans to be rolled up to group level and then all groups can be consolidated to total company level. A clear picture of the financial requirements to run the business is thereby provided to senior management and enables the arrangements for the liquidity of funds necessary for each month.

Using the values from the intake plan above the financial planning summary will look as follows

DEPARTMENTAL MONTHLY FINANCIAL SUMMARY

	OPEN STOCK	SALES	MARKDOWN	INTAKE	CLOSE STOCK
MONTH 1	77 000	50 000	700	54 700	81 000
MONTH 2	81 000	54 000		71 000	98 000
MONTH 3	98 000	83 000		67 000	82 000
MONTH 4	82 000	54 000		46 200	85 000
MONTH 5	85 000	59 000		70 000	83 000
MONTH 6	83 000	56 000		56 000	83 000

The determination of intake required is applicable at any product hierarchy level. The highest platform would be for the total company which then cascades down to group and department. Thereafter it can be drilled down to product level and subsequently to colour and size.

The same holds true for location planning from total company through to regional and store level.

The principle of top down planning and bottom up verification is key to accurate forecasting. Experience shows that should planning be done from bottom up with a consolidation to a higher level, it is inevitable that the original overall top level plan will be exceeded. If each line is considered in isolation, the reality of the influencing factors such as late deliveries, unforeseen obstacles and events are discounted and will therefore invariably deliver a much more optimistic plan. The added danger of a bottom up approach could possibly result in uncertainty or mistrust of the strategy and therefore plans with excessive percentage increases on last year should be challenged and be given careful consideration and validation.

A point to remember is that budgets cannot be banked and there seems to be a natural tendency of human nature to be optimistic and endeavour to justify higher budget levels. It is important to remain as realistic as possible in the setting of the financial plan levels.

The challenge of chasing products where performance is above expectation is far more pleasurable than frantically switching off production and suffering the consequences of over commitments which may be in the form of completed product or raw materials. The threat of suppliers having to work shorter hours or needing to retrench production staff can also become a real possibility.

Plans should be realistic in terms of the transition from a preceding season into a new season. Formulating budgets in isolation comes with the dogged assumption that the errors of the previous season will not be repeated nor will there be any misjudgements going forward. The expectation is also that the benefits which will be enjoyed through new initiatives and products are over and above current levels of performance. The reality is however that this does not happen from day one when at midnight of the last day of the previous season the mediocre level of sales will instantly transform into a higher optimistic level of performance almost as if a message was shot off to all customers to tell them to start buying more.

Another common trap is that during the formulation of the strategy and operational plan the desires are considered to be a given and it is assumed without doubt that it is going to happen. A common example is the want to generate higher levels of profit which may be done through the adjustment of the margin policy upwards and inevitably selling prices as well. It is presumed that the change will be happily accepted by customers and intake plans are then put in place to meet the revised targets. The unfortunate inevitability is that the changeover does not happen immediately from day one of the new season as it takes a time for customers to digest and possibly modify buying habits. Consequently disillusionment amongst the retail team reigns which results in strategy and sales plans being questioned and a resultant panic plan to rectify the situation is implemented at an early stage.

During the trading period the actual values will differ to the planned expectations and the anticipated values need to be substituted with the actual. The plan going forward consequently needs to be adjusted based on a different opening stock, changed markdown value and therefore requires that the intake value to be adjusted in order to bring the plan back in line.

Where performance is not up to standard, the product mix of the intake going forward may still remain well-matched to the plan in terms of any new coordinated ranges and seasonal launches. In order to ensure that this is done effectively it could be necessary to consider other options whereby stock levels may be allowed to drift above planned levels for a time and to be gradually brought back in line to realistic targets.

A worthy practice is to permit for spare open to buy right up to the latest point in time before committing in contract form. Such a tactic will facilitate the pursuit of the better selling lines or being able to absorb growing overstocks thus maintaining tighter stock controls and avoiding possible financial disaster.

Integration of hierarchy level plans

Product plans from a company level down to individual product group by week need to be integrated with the location planning hierarchy in order that the stores are stocked with the most appropriate assortment of product to effectively satisfy the customer needs.

The same principle applies in location plans that the higher hierarchical levels are considered to be the most accurate to lay down the parameters to which plans from the lower levels are balanced back to.

The integration of plans is illustrated below

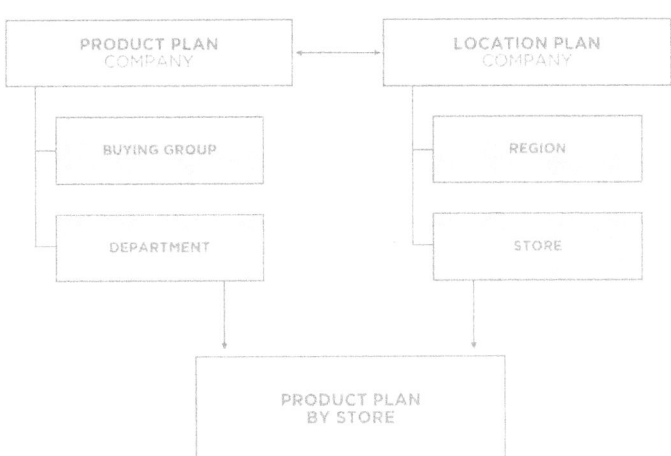

Location plans

In setting up the location plans it is important to be aware of what products are going to which stores and be sure that they are in suitable proportions and quantities that will best service the unique customer profiles that are applicable to the individual stores. The store profile or personality will be influenced predominantly by the surrounding economic factors, lifestyles and cultural demographics. A common technique to consider is to group similar profile stores into specific groupings so that they all carry like catalogues of products which will assist in the efficiency of planning and achieve a comparable handwriting across the chain.

A logical way to define the accurate range of product types as well as give guidance to the quantities for the right places is through the drafting of a matrix which indicates the correct kind of products that are to be destined to different groups of stores. In principle there is a base selection of product that would go to all stores and thereafter selected products which will be earmarked for specific store profile groups dependent on factors such as sales budgets, space constraints, layout plans, price sensitivity and fashion demands.

A simple example of such a matrix could look as follows.

DEPARTMENT XYZ	STORE PROFILE Group A	STORE PROFILE Group B	STORE PROFILE Group C	STORE PROFILE Group D	STORE PROFILE Group E
PRODUCT 1	X	X	X	X	X
PRODUCT 2	X	X	X	X	X
PRODUCT 3	X	X	X	X	X
PRODUCT 4	X	X	X	X	X
PRODUCT 5	X	X	X	X	X
PRODUCT 6	X	X	X		
PRODUCT 7	X	X	X	X	
PRODUCT 8	X	X			
PRODUCT 9	X	X			X
PRODUCT 10	X				

An underlying standard which needs to be understood is that planning is a constantly changing iterative process that requires continual pre-season and in-season review dependent on customers, competitors and suppliers behaving differently to what was anticipated.

The eighty twenty rule

A point of consideration that should never be ignored is the eighty twenty rule, also known as the Pareto principle where it is acknowledged that eighty percent of the result is delivered by twenty percent of the effort or participants.

In the context of stores it is probable that twenty percent of the stores deliver eighty percent of the sales and deserve the proportionate dedication of energy and focus, as does the thick middle sizes such as medium and large and therefore should always be in stock. Core base colours such as white, black, naturals and greys also contribute largely to the sales and should always be evident in volume. It is clear that certain styling features will likewise guarantee the bulk of sales and should be finalised first and certain peak trading periods such as holidays or special events will contribute largely to the total seasonal sales and must be managed very carefully in terms of production planning and delivery scheduling.

It should be qualified that it is not necessarily exactly a ratio of eighty versus twenty as in certain cases it could be a ninety to ten or seventy to thirty relationship but nevertheless the principle still holds true.

BUYING

Department line sales summary

Prior to the building of the range or buying plan there must be an indication of the expected item sales in money value and units as well as the relative proportion splits across the range for the various store catalogues with the relative variances between this year and last year for the sales value, units and price which will all serve as the preliminary basis for discussion and provide the guidance for the formulation of the intake and range plan.

Price moves highlight whether the inflationary indications are at acceptable levels particularly where products are identical to the previous year and the like for like percentage move is at least in line or is less than the consumer price index.

An example of a line by line summary is as follows

PROD NO	DESCRIPTION	STORE CATALOGUE	SELLING PRICE			SALES '000			SALES UNITS		
			LY	TY	% inc/dec	LY	TY	% inc/dec	LY	TY	% inc/dec
	PROD GROUP 1										
1001	Style ABCD	A4	95.00	99.99	5.2%	680 000	730 000	5.7%	7 168	7 300	2.0%
2001	Style ABCE	A4	125.00	128.99	4.0%	500 000	550 000	10.0%	4 000	4 231	5.7%
	PROD GROUP 2										
1002	Style ABCF	A4	175.00	180.00	2.9%	299 000	350 000	17.0%	1 708	1 944	13.8%
2002	Style ABCG	A4	175.00	180.00	2.9%	345 000	400 000	15.9%	1 971	2 222	12.8%
3001	Style ABCH	A4	175.00	180.00	2.9%	365 000	390 000	6.8%	2 085	2 027	9.7%
TOTAL DEPARTMENT			129.40	136.53	5.5%	2 189 000	2 420 000	10.6%	16 922	17 724	4.7%

Building the range plan

The construction of a range plan may commence once the financial targets are available through the product and store plans together with a store catalogue matrix. The range plan enables the drafting of a so called "shopping list" for the buying team to be able to fill in the blanks as they make their selections.

The purpose of the range plan is to ensure that the offer of commercial and all-inclusive product ranges meet the needs of all customers. This is done through the combination of the elements of science which covers the planning aspect and art that represents the buying function. To expand further, the scientific practice delivers the clarity of the range offer, the quantities of style and colour levels with the correct pricing policies that support structured cataloguing which meet the varying customer profile pools. The artistic involvement delivers beautiful product and style in categories offering real choice in a way that they are easy to shop. The determination to achieve a successful balanced combination will assist in the potential maximisation of sales and profit as well as undoubtedly help to grow market share.

The philosophies of building a range is the procedure of analysing the historical sales of product categories as well as heeding the lessons learnt from previous seasons and being guided by the strategic definitions. Modifications to the current range structures could be done to compensate for missed opportunities, lost sales through uncommon adversities should be accounted for as is the need to cater for inflated sales as a result of upcoming out of the norm special events.

A balance of the right product mix between the basic range types and the fashion inputs has to be determined. The large volume items should be the first focus to ensure that the relevant high money takers are looked after adequately. Second is the necessity to correctly identify the characteristics of fashion forward goods for each product category in order that they best meet the respective store groupings customer profiles and reflect good relative value to other internal or external products.

The end goal is best summarised by the well-worn quote of having the right product at the right time in the right place at the right price in the right quantities.

A simple range plan model based on the guidelines reflected in the departmental line summary above is illustrated on the next page.

Department XYZ Range Plan

Product Group	Style	Colour	Stores	Cost /Input	Cost price	Sell price	Intake margin	Intake sell value	Intake units	Month 1 Week 1	Week 2	Week 3	Week 4	Month 2 Week 5	Week 6	Week 7	Week 8	Month 3 Week 9	Week 10	Week 11	Week 12	Week 13
1000	White	All	Cost	46.99	99.99	51%	2500000	25000	2500	140	175	230	225	115	175	200	275	350	250	350	861	250
	Black	Cost	Gep A,B,C	46.99	99.99	55%	1800000	1800		120	175	160	180	100	140	210	270	120	160	140		200
	Blue	Cost	All	46.99	99.99	53%	1200000	1200		112	64	128	144	12	96	128	176	96	96	112		160
2001	Purple	All	Cost	46.99	29.99	51%	2000000			64	96	96	108	60	84	96	132	96	64			
	Beige	Cost	All	63.69	29.99	51%	3500000	3500		138	162	165	206	75	162	165	254	185	185			
	White	Cost	All	63.69	29.99	51%	2400000			162	135	154		86	154	154	212	136	162			
	Green	Cost	Gep A	63.69	29.99	57%	1000000			46	46	64	61	38	46	61	84	61				

Product group 1				Intake units						2500												
				Intake selling value																		
				Merchandise intake plan																		

2	1001	Purple	All	Input	82.81	180	54%	1800000	818	715	861	125	1127	815	886	738	994	984	2584	861	2250
	Yellow	Gep A,B	Input	82.81	180	54%	1800000	987												
2002	Orange	All	Input	52.81	180	54%	600000	644	578		67									
	Pink	All	Input	82.81	180	54%	1700000	944												
	Brown	All	Input	82.81	180	54%	1400000	778				905		142		497		104		
3000	Black	Gep A,B	Input	82.81	180	54%	1900000	1046				660		117		603		147		
	Green	All	Input	82.81	180	54%	1000000	556				472		84		614		108		
	White	All	Input	82.81	180	54%	1700000	944												
	Grey	Gep A,B	Input	82.81	160	54%	1300000	722												

Product group 2				Intake units						1903				1936				2134				
				Intake selling value																		
				Merchandise intake plan																		

3	1003	Purple	All	Input	103.42	230	55%	1950000	682	580		102		485		135		854		538	
	Yellow	All	Input	103.42	230	55%	1700000	775	657		186			76		685		123		
	Orange	Gep A,B	Input	103.42	230	53%	1200000	546	464		82			150		667		116		
2003	Pink	All	Input	103.42	230	53%	1800000	778				162				497				
	Brown	All	Input	103.42	230	55%	1900000	864				734		89		685				
3003	Black	Gep A,B	Input	103.42	230	53%	1900000	901				502				423		121		
	Green	All	Input	103.42	230	53%	1800000	808										116		
	White	All	Input	103.42	230	53%	1700000	743										49		
	Grey	Gep A,B	Input	103.42	230	53%	1600000	701												

Product group 3				Intake units						7370		370		1853		135		1854		538	
				Intake selling value		1470000				374230	65300		485300	73900		408000	720900				
				Merchandise intake plan		1480000				374000	65900		408500	73450		408020	72100				

Total Dept XYZ				Intake units					29650	4292	867	1673	1057	4444	861	1658	1833	4906	964	1720	861	2250
				Intake selling value					40420700	7541200	964600	7271900	1241100	8145000	961600	2454400	1501800	9473000	1100600	2559000	966600	15500.00
				Merchandise intake plan					40407000	7543440	966157	2267400	1242345	8134905	965755	2454500	1508355	9497350	1101140	1951144	968435	13890.50

The model assumes the following.

The plan is for a department that has one continuity product group and two product groups for input fashion styles.

The catalogue makes a provision to keep in line with the product and location matrix plan.

The shape of intake across time is regulated as per the shape reflected in the merchandise sales plan.

The period being planned is for three months of a six month season.

The merchandise intake plan row is included for a direct comparison to the merchandise plan intake values for easy reconciliation to ensure that the planned buy is in line with the financial intention.

The intake margin column enables the continual monitor to ensure that the target intake margin is on track with that as deemed to be in the strategy.

The closing stock is determined using the weeks forward cover and therefore takes into account the sales values of the first few weeks in the next phase in order to calculate the closing stocks towards the latter part of the season.

The volumes of the inputs are those that are required to service the catalogue and be on offer for sale until replenished by the next style input. As in the example it is wise to keep a second smaller input to replenish initial sales as some stores will sell out quicker or slower than expected. If the full quantity is put in all at once there could be a situation where there will be pockets of stock left over which will increase the potential of mark downs while on the other hand probable sales will be lost in those stores that are depleted of stock.

The offer for sales time period is determined by the frequency of inputs. In the example above the inputs are the monthly themes and the sales period that are attributed to each style will be for six weeks after which any leftover stocks will be destined for the reduced counters or racks.

Volume and choice balance

The creation of the initial range plan reflects the quantities that have to be bought at item level by colour, in the correct size ranges, at the target mark-ups and retail selling prices. It is essential that the monetary buying amounts of the plan are aligned to the merchandise plan intake values.

The buying plan should reflect the strategy which guarantees the correct amount of selection within the stock parameters while still providing the right spread of products in the required quantities that will best serve the target customer in both style, form and function at any point in time of the season.

During the construction of the plan, the principle that needs to be adhered to is that the merchandise plan must guide the buy with the customer top of mind. Lessons learnt from previous seasons need to be analysed and equally applied to both the basic continuity lines as well as the high end fashion products. Fundamentally it is also important to get the right balance of the correct number of choices in quantities that enable the guarantee of basic lines in depth without impeding the introduction of newness.

It happens often that too much emphasis is placed on the fringe or peripheral lines, or there is excessive similarity in characteristics and price offerings that can disrupt the balance. The emotional wishes of the buying team and suppliers can also have an influence on a distorted balance being achieved and should be guarded against.

The range plan which represents the assortment of products developed within specific categories must represent the organisation of the business and therefore should be balanced across the width and depth of the structure.

The width represents how broad the choice of product is while the depth represents the quantities required to cover the number of sizes and colours including the amount of price points within the product categories. It is probably easier for niche retailers that focus on a narrower customer segment of the market to best be able to serve the both the depth and width demands of their market.

The difficulties that retailers are faced with in striking the right balance of width and depth of ranges is that of presenting real customer choice while at same time optimising the return on investment. In other words, there is the need to attract customers by maintaining a level of newness and fashionability without compromising the traditional or core customers and especially the high volume sellers. It is therefore critical that the buyer has a clear vision of the marketing position and understands the target customer though continuous research which provides the confidence to determine as to what should or should not be kept in the range.

The volume and choice balance emphasis that the customer expects to find new styles in their size in a variety of colours can be illustrated as follows.

Style and shape proportions

The styles that will make up the range structure are dictated by history, the strategy guidelines and direction provided by the design or trend teams.

If one considers the thought process of a customer when a selection is being made, the first feature that she will

114

be attracted to is the style. If the style does not meet the required taste level it will be ignored. The criteria that will influence this choice may not necessarily be the level of fashionability but also the practicality of the garment in meeting the required functionality, examples of which are sleeve lengths, belted or unbelted waists, lengths, neckline or any other feature that will allow the customer to feel comfortable and confident to wear.

Multiple choices form the basis of range plan structure and ensure that all customer preferences are catered for. Another need that has to be provided for is the availability of styling and colours that can be easily coordinated with other product styles within the same or other departments.

Consideration also needs to be given to the cross co-ordination of fashionable items being supported by core product. An example would be a fashion blouse including the core shades in the design or print that would go happily with a basic core skirt in complimentary fabric types. The implementation of this strategy is important as too much deviation from the core pillars will reduce the product relevance and could result in a deterioration of market penetration.

Pricing structure

It is absolutely essential to consider the structure or architecture of pricing across the range in order that a consistent balance is maintained between the good value, mid and luxury price points. Added to this is the controlling of the price movement from one season to the next. The rate of increases or decreases need to be measured on a like for like basis whereby the change in price of identical products is compared to an acceptable overall rate such as the consumer price index while still maintaining the margin targets. Other products should also represent good value in comparison to similar products in the market place.

The philosophy and pricing strategy of the retailer will dictate the balance of price groups dependent on the customer segments that they serve. Probable examples would be where a discount value chain will have about ninety percent of product in the low value band while the middle price type of retailer will have possibly forty percent low price goods with the bulk of products falling into the mid-price range at about fifty five percent. Top end luxury retailers will commonly have in excess of ninety percent of prices falling in the high price range.

A pitfall that needs to be avoided is a scenario where critical price points are maintained through harsh negotiation tactics for more than one or two seasons as it could happen that it will eventually reach a point that without an increase it may become no longer viable for the supplier to manufacture. A decision to then move the price to a realistic level could result in the customer resisting the purchase as a result of the perception that the price is excessive in relation to the previous season. Credibility may also be lost as there may be great difficulty in justifying the narrower gap difference between other products within the range and they in turn could be interpreted to represent poor value.

Extreme deep cut promotions may have a similar impact and the danger exists that the balance of the margins may become distorted. An overall anticipated intake margin is based on planned quantities but in reality is rapidly lessened where repetitive turn-ons of the lower margin product takes place.

A factor that must be considered is the effect of the price movement on unit volumes and whether or not the reduced quantities will still service the store catalogue sufficiently to maintain good continuity. If this is not the case it may require the rationalisation of the number of customer choices offered or a restriction of the store catalogue for the product.

A tactic that retailers frequently resort to in terms of a psychological influence is the selection of the number of price points as well as the pricing terminology. For this reason price points such as 99.00 presents a better perception of value than if the product was marked 100.00. This technique however must be handled with caution as for high ticketed items it is better to present 300.00 rather than 299.00 as this may deliver a message of perceived deviousness. In terms of the gaps between price points, the wider they are among the product groups the better is the value perception. In cases where the customer is bombarded with too many price options it becomes increasingly difficult to assess the value variance between products.

Retailers sometimes apply regional pricing where the income status of customers differ. The result is that customers in the poorer areas enjoy a discount that is subsidised by those in the more affluent areas. Similarly there are unscrupulous retailers who launch a product at an unrealistic high price and after a short period reduce it to a price that delivers a normal margin but is promoted aggressively as great value. These practices once exposed are not well received by consumers and become great topics of discussion on social media.

Colour range

The second determining feature of the product that will influence the purchasing decision will be the colour. Colour is the first element of newness and trend direction that is displayed. Many season's ranges can fail through poor interpretation of the seasonal colour trend. How the colour themes are flowed across the seasons is important as is the harmony that exists with not only the colours within each individual product range but also with the overall look of the store. The visual impact is important in that it transmits a subliminal message to the customer through a fine balance of fashion colours to those that the customer prefers.

Core colours should be banked first even though they may not always be the most exciting. A wise retailer once said "white is a business" and this certainly holds true for black, grey, navy, beige and brown year in and year out. The trending themes such as lilacs, pinks, yellows are more often than not linked to the prevailing trends and will dictate the seasonal themes from month to month. There is a place for the high risk edgy colours such funky pinks, shocking purples and burnt oranges as they provide the theatre even though they may not deliver the best returns.

In order to achieve the best variety it is important to ensure that the planned colour spectrum is reflected as a whole by assigning different colours across the diverse styles in the range with the overall proportions meeting the targets of the strategic intent.

Examining the table below it is evident that the plan is not aligned to the strategic target and therefore a revisit to the proportions will be required to bring them in line with the objective.

NUMBER	COLOUR	UNITS	LY	UNITS PLANNED	TY	TY TARGET
1	White	250	19%	356	25%	28%
2	Black	430	33%	356	25%	25%
3	Stone	130	10%	178	13%	15%
4	Khaki	200	15%	178	13%	12%
5	Red	250	19%	178	13%	10%
6	Pink	40	3%	178	13%	10%
	TOTAL	1 300	100%	1 424	100%	100%

Size architecture

As has been highlighted previously, the first attractor to the customer is the style and then colour but the reality remains that the choice will only be complete if the size is available in the wanted style and colour. For this reason many retailers will display their offerings by size so as to minimize the frustration that results when the size is not available in the desired style and colour.

The need to minimise the non-availability of particular sizes is the main reason as to why special attention should be paid to the careful planning and analysis of size profiles.

It is logical that stores have differing size profiles which are driven by the local demographics, shopping patterns and cultural preferences. For this reason the product groupings and styling features need to be carefully assessed. Typical examples would be that possibly in the rural areas customers may be genetically of a larger stature than their counterparts in the cities and could also have a more conservative attitude than the adventurous city slickers. Religious beliefs may also have an influence where certain parts of the body such as arms need to be covered.

As with the top down and bottom up merchandise planning principle we need to determine the overall national size curve for a department, product category and product in order to place the full combined order with the supplier.

Similarly the accumulated store size profiles have to be derived and aligned with the product size profile in order that allocations can meet both the product and store needs.

The size analysis for small, medium and large emphasis size stores will require differing size ratios for each group.

By way of illustration

The department requires total of 6200 units. Based on historical and trend analysis the target size ratio will represent.

	SMALL	MEDIUM	LARGE	X-LARGE
SIZE RATIO %	16%	24%	40%	20%
TOTAL ORDER	1 000	1 500	2 500	1 500

There are three product styles which may or may not be ordered from the same supplier but each will be in the form of a separate order or contract. Because of the different characteristics of each style, the size ratio requirements may be different.

The quantities in the table below will reflect these separate style orders

STYLE	SMALL	MEDIUM	LARGE	X-LARGE
STYLE A (basic for average customer)	300	500	600	400
% RATIO	17%	28%	33%	22%
STYLE B (larger for fuller figure)	200	600	1 100	800
% RATIO	8%	22%	40%	30%
STYLE C (petite high fashion style)	600	900	400	200
% RATIO	29%	43%	19%	9%
TOTAL	1 100	2 000	2 100	1 400
% RATIO	17%	30%	32%	21%

It is not uncommon in women's sizing designed to fit diverse body shapes to carry different descriptive names. Such variations include the height of a person dependent on the torso or back length, whether the bust, waist and hips are straighter which is usually more relevant to teenagers or curvier for mostly adult women.

Examples of such descriptive categories are commonly misses sizes, junior sizes, women's or plus sizes, petite, junior petite and the like.

In order to cater for the varying size silhouettes of individual stores the relevant size ratios pertaining to the particular stores have to be applied. A practical way of doing this can be done by grouping stores with similar size profiles together and utilise these groupings for planned allocations.

A simple working example is outlined below.

Style A – Basic for average customer

Total units are 1800 units

Assume that the total proportions for the store groupings are

Small size emphasis stores units	25%	440
Medium size emphasis stores units	55%	990
Large size emphasis stores units	20%	370

Based on historical analysis and trend assessment assume that size % splits across the size range for the various store size profiles will be as follows.

	Small	Medium	Large	X-Large
Small size emphasis stores	22%	27%	32%	19%
Medium size emphasis stores	15%	31%	32%	22%

Large size emphasis stores   13%

21%   37%   29%

The results displayed in the table below reflects in what proportions the total ordered quantity of 1800 will be allocated to meet the size profiles of the individual stores.

	SMALL	MEDIUM	LARGE	X-LARGE
SMALL EMPHASIS STORES	97	119	140	85
SIZE RATIO	22%	27%	32%	19%
MEDIUM EMPHASIS STORES	153	305	320	209
SIZE RATIO	15%	31%	32%	22%
LARGE EMPHASIS STORES	50	76	140	106
SIZE RATIO	13%	21%	37%	29%
TOTAL	300	500	600	379
SIZE RATIO	17%	28%	33%	22%

123

A typical overall size curve can be illustrated using a Bell type curve

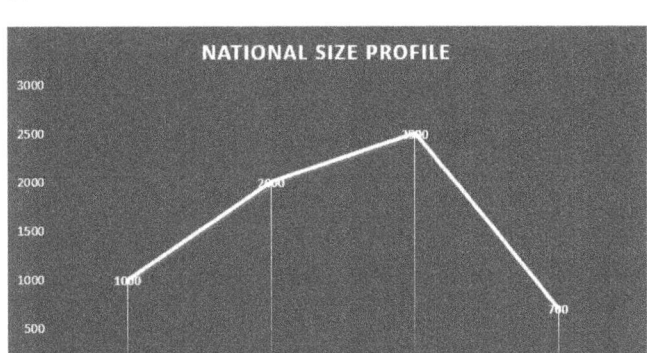

While the above represents the overall size curve this will have to be equivalent to the sum of the individual product categories size curves.

For simplicity we can assume that this overall curve is made up of three product types which are a basic type with medium size emphasis, a style for the fuller figure and a high fashion smaller size emphasis requirement. These in turn need to service stores that are size small emphasis, size medium emphasis and size large emphasis profiles.

In conclusion a check list should be drafted which confirms that all the deliverables expected from the range plan are adequately covered. These would include the confirmation of the presence of key looks and trends for the season, that all the end use options are available for the customer, that the range has a look of freshness, the assortment includes the expect to find products and does not contain any duplications.

Validation is required to ensure that the strategic intents of the product group, supplier, sourcing team and designers have been met and lastly that the margin target is achieved.

The use of trials

The trusted use of trial quantities which can be put into stores prior to the season may be intended to test attributes such as styling, colours, prints, fabrics, fashion looks, technical or innovative direction or even a value added feature such as a detachable hood in order to gauge the potential of a market.

The trial must also be specific as to what is being tested and it is not advisable to combine different features at the same time. For example, if the purpose is to test a colour, it should be done in a tried and tested style rather than using a new concept style. If this is not done, it could lead to a confused result as to whether it was the style that was successful or was it because of the colour that sales were disappointing.

In order to get a realistic reading of the potential of an untested product it is important to utilise the stores that represent the target market across the chain rather than simply using the larger stores in an environment where there is all likelihood of selling. It is preferred to use a selected cross section of stores and compare performance against similar control styles in the same stores and then extrapolate the results to all stores in the intended catalogue to determine the overall sales potential of the trial product.

Where open to buy is restricted, which is almost always the case, a recommended tactic is to hive off an amount upfront which will allow the freedom to experiment at any time and potentially grow a high volume line.

Range presentations

It is only natural that before the final go-ahead to commit to production is given that the intended range for the forthcoming season is presented to the senior management of a retail organisation in order to get their views, buy in and sign off as a combined decision making unit.

Prior to the commencement of the season it is normal that the design team briefs management and buying groups of key looks, colour themes and other relevant trends for the forthcoming season, while the post seasonal analysis is presented by the commercial team of the buying groups to highlight some of the key lessons learnt from the previous season's trading. The commercial arm will also get approval of proposed budget levels and strategy intents from senior management to ensure that all are aligned in thinking before going ahead with the planning process and the range build.

The range presentations can take on varying formats but in the main the end objective remains the same in that all stakeholders must be comfortable with the selections and strategies to maximise the sales and profit potential.

The attendees who would participate would normally be senior management and the representitives of the relevant buying teams being the category managers, buyers, merchandisers, technologists, location planners, allocators, marketing team, store representitives, members of the design team and supply chain or logistical representitives all of whom may well make contributions where appropriate.

Typical contributions are where the technologists may describe new innovations, the garment technologists or sourcing specialists could discuss supplier issues and describe new suppliers, a store representitive will add comment as to possibly the practicality of styling based on what they have gleened through their interaction with customers, location planners will confirm that the quantities being purchased are sufficient to serve the designated catalogue or will accommodate the volumes required for planned promotions as outlined by marketing.

The agenda is usually commenced with an overall summary by the category manager of the strategy which will refer to supplier sourcing, technological developments, pricing policies, key looks and themes and lessons learnt from the previous year which have been taken on board.

The presentation of the numbers side of the department is done by the merchandiser using the line by line department summary as a point of reference. The main points that are highlighted will be the budget levels emphasising the performance in comparison to last year as well as the proportions of each product category with special attention being given to the splits between the automatic replenishment type product and the more fashionable input lines which will carry the newness and represent the more exciting part of the range.

It is usually with regard to this that some form of clarification may be required where levels tend to deviate from the norm. An example of this may well be reflected in increases that are excessive but are justified possibly by a new initiative or increase in store catalogue that is being introduced. What must be guarded against is that the level of increase of the continuity lines tends to be set more conservatively as the assumption is made that they can grow to a level which will be greater than the budget because the raw material requirement is placed ahead of time. The temptation is thereby to free up funds to enable the introduction or addition of the more fashionable product which will not be as easy to turn on. Technically if thought is applied to this practice, it is nothing else but a disguised form of over buying.

Another point needs to be made with reference to the practice of funding the input fashion lines from the surplus created by the conservative budgeting of continuity lines. If this tactic is employed it will result in the distortion of the buying margin. The reality is that the continuity lines will probably sell at higher levels than budgeted but as they carry more conservative margins the actual overall margin will be less than that which was presented.

Other aspects that will be referred to is the unit increases in relation to last year and comments will be made about the overall increase or decrease in percentage terms and differentiation will be made between the like for like product price movements which should be referenced to the current consumer price index.

The profit margins will be discussed to ensure that the profit objectives are met taking into account the levels of mark downs planned and confirming the reality of these amounts based on historical performance.

The attribute splits need to be confirmed such as short sleeves versus long sleeves, collar versus non collar, tops compared to bottoms, colour ratios, size characteristics, wovens versus knitted goods, the fabric type splits and the like.

While the number part of the meeting is often seen as the dull and boring bit with very little exciting exposure to the actual product it nevertheless remains probably the most important part of setting the business end foundation and should be given the attention to detail that is deserved.

Once the numbers have been agreed and all team members are comfortable, the buyer will proceed to present the product that is going to make up the range which is going to deliver the budgetry objectives. The most conveniant way is to first display the continuity product that will flow through for the entire season and then drop in the monthly inputs which will emphasise the themes in terms of styling and colour for each relevant month. It is also important to check that the specific looks tie in with the other departments complementry product to ensure themes are aligned.

The products display the detail pertaining to the garment on an attached card such as the quantity being purchased, the catalogue of the stores that they are destined for, the selling price and margin and colours with corresponding swatches. Where possible the product should be in the actual material and make up that will be representitive of what will be seen in stores.

It may have to be that for product which is earmarked for a latter part of the seasons that CAD boards will have to suffice.

In the presentation of the range by month a recommended tactic would be to build the look by store catalogue where the smaller stores range will be displayed first and ticked off and then followed by what the next band of stores will receive untill the full range which the flagship stores will carry is displayed. In this way the range across the full chain can be envisaged and attendees are not misled into thinking that the look of the entire range is going to all stores.

As with other meetings the conclusions should be noted, actions listed with time deadlines attached and an accountability component included. This note should be circulated to all attendees and kept on file to serve as a point of reference should there be disagreement when the actual goods reach the sales floor and they are not remembered as the same that was signed off.

Store range profiling

The differing customer profiles of individual stores is not limited to the size profiles but requires a skilled knowledge of the stores in order that complete customer needs are optimally serviced.

In the main the responsibility rests with the planner while in some organisations there may be dedicated location planners who will study the key attributes of stores in conjunction with the sales and management staff within the stores. This is often a point that is overlooked as it is easy to be too defensive as to the reasons why certain products have not performed to expectation. An objective separate view from those who interact at the coalface with the customer places the reality of the situation in perspective.

Not all stores will be able to stock everything and the catalogues need to flex to best meet the demand for the customer that is served by the particular store.

What is important to note is that the sum of the location plans from individual store to total company need to be in line with the total merchandise plans which are reconciled to the overall buy.

In terms of the forward cover requirements of stores they are dependent on the rate of turnover that the stores enjoy. In principle the high turnover larger stores will tend to have lower forward covers as they need less stock in relation to the volume of sales to maintain effective levels of display whereas at the other end of the scale the smaller low turnover stores which require more stock in relation to their sales to maintain the availability of all sizes and colours all of the time and thus will be replenished less frequently. The typical relationship would be that the larger stores will require in the region of five weeks forward cover whereas the smaller stores may need ten weeks of forward sales to present full availability to the customers. For this reason and the physical constraints it is likely that the smaller stores will carry a lesser number of styles in the catalogue in comparison to the larger units.

The catalogue of the store will be influenced by the demographics, income bands and cultural factors. The process that the location planner will follow when assessing a store is firstly to review the sales levels of the various categories of product and examine those areas where there have been unacceptable levels of markdown and probe the reasons why this has occurred which may result in a decision to remove certain categories. Conversely missed opportunities need to be identified and action plans drafted to ensure that these are optimised going forward.

It is unlikely that the sales shape across time for every store is going to match that of the overall company. A prime example is a coastal resort store will experience seasonal peak sales during holiday periods while will be extremely conservative outside these times or conversely stores will experience depressed sales in university towns where there is an exodus of students during the holiday period.

The frequently recommended approach is to plan each store as if it is your only store. This is however easier said than done particularly where some chain stores may have hundreds of stores. In many cases the control of stocks at micro level can be extremely time consuming and complex but the use of technical software packages have made it possible to accurately measure sales performance and determine stock requirements to the finest detail based on historical sales patterns.

New stores need to be reviewed as the sales shape may be distorted by the initial opening hype or the fact that it may have been only partially open for the period under review. A common approach that is adopted to plan the range selection for new or refurbished stores is to mirror them to a similar profile store and base the quantities on a comparable turnover size store.

Where sales are disappointingly low it might require the de-cataloguing of certain lines or certain sizes of a specific offering in order to minimise markdowns without disappointing a large section of customers and enabling the freeing up of more space to expose good performing ranges more forcefully.

A scenario could exist where stores require a wider assortment of product in lesser quantities. The obvious influencing factors in the main will be space constraints, the changing demographics of the town, the store may have been modernized or a new mall may have opened or closed all of which would justify a wider assortment.

The effective utilisation of space in a store is determined by the percentage sales contribution of each product category. Strategically this may be deviated from, examples of which are where a possible focus is required on a new range launch or because of a younger customer age demographic who have more children will inspire a thrust to aggressively feature children's ranges. In principle these deviations must be carefully considered so that the other product groupings are not placed in danger of being stifled entirely.

The measurement of space is translated into facings or opportunities for the customers to choose from with relevant appropriate values attached for shelves, rails, pegs, table displays in conjunction with the equipment positioning. In other words, a rail in the darkest back corner of the store will carry less value to that on the entry aisle at the front door of the store which enjoys the greatest traffic flow. The placement of total departments will follow the same principle where the highest turnover departments will enjoy the more prominent positioning with greater exposure.

The layout of the store should facilitate a journey through the store from one area to another interlaced with co-ordinated displays suggesting to the customer options to consider for a complete wardrobe option including apparel, accessories and impulse products before they reach the pay points. Layouts that are static straight up and down rows fail to entice customers to other areas of the store.

STOCK MANAGEMENT

The efficient management of stock is frequently neglected. The inclination is to believe that the more sold, the greater is the profit. While this is true, without the careful management of stock holdings the profit benefit can easily be eradicated. There are a number of reasons for this but it cannot be emphasized enough that constant attention is required to ensure that potential profits are not quickly eroded either through sell outs or overstocks.

The first sign of poor sales of a style is often optimistically justified by assuming that things will get better and the conclusion is too easily arrived at that it is merely a temporary setback. Good examples are thinking that the weather is not quite right, a big event has occupied the customer's minds, and the customer does not understand the product or a competitor had a killer sale at the same time. Inevitably this procrastination of corrective behaviour results in the point of no return being reached and by the time reality sets in, the consequent punishment in the form of higher markdowns could be the result.

Another common trap is that when sales are sluggish to throw more stock at the problem. Store management often justify poor performance by routinely stating that they do not have enough stock. However, upon examination, it is found more often than not that this is not the case and more intense probing needs to be conducted.

Stockholdings must be kept as tight as possible and where essential, the rationalisation through the elimination of fringe sizes and colours or whole ranges from the store catalogue will keep forward covers to a minimum and improve stock turns.

Promotional activity in whatever form that is appropriate can also help to alleviate the situation. Such price cuts or offers must be meaningful and albeit at lower margins, the removal of stock allows the inflow of newer fresh socks together with the freeing up of display area and does not force the banishment of goods to storage possibly never to see the light of day again until the major clearance sales.

Contingency plans should be put in place such as turning off production of slow selling styles, converting the style into more successful shapes and if the problem lies with the colour or fabrication it is better to take the write down on fabric rather than in garment form.

In this day and age where the accuracy of stock data bases is reliant on the efficiency of the information technology systems, the correct labelling of product is absolutely essential so that the precise data is captured which is critical for the effective replenishment of the product.

Pilferage, shop spoilage, customer returns of poor quality products, incorrect stock counts, visual display garments and goodwill donations are part and parcel of the retail environment and such product is rendered unsaleable but remains on the stock records which then distorts the replenishment needs. Stock adjustments are normally done by store staff and as a result the human error factor is very real as well as the manipulation of records is tempting to guarantee a flattering lower shrinkage result.

The more basic continuity lines that are on display for long periods of time are most susceptible to stock inaccuracies. A revealing sign of such a situation may be where stocks are reflected week after week but do not have any corresponding sales on performance documents. The impact of these false positive records is often evident that when sales slowdown of such a style and a new injection of goods with a different stock keeping record suddenly delivers a much improved sales performance.

Some retailers apply a technique of stock ageing where goods are date coded and after a reasonable period of time a particular date code can be considered as phantom or odds and ends and are flushed out by deleting them from the stock record data base.

Fashion input styles may also be date coded and are flagged for price reduction at a point in time when the styles or colours are no longer relevant to the prevailing trends or themes. For this reason the incorporation of date codes in the barcode assists in the correct rotation of stock whereby the older dated stock is sold first but this requires well controlled stock rotation disciplines in warehouses and stores.

The converse situation where the stocks are supposedly non-existent is not as serious as it may still be available for sale. The real impact is dependent on the size of the error as the non-existence of records of stock will attract a need to be replaced and could lead to potential overstocks.

The maintenance of accurate stock data is dependent largely on the well regimented stock takes as in spite of the belief that continual cyclical counts will keep physical stocks in line with theoretical records, the truth is that often these deliver greater inaccuracies as they are not as disciplined and often misplaced stocks, duplicate displays and soiled goods are excluded from counts. Added to this regular stock counts come with extra costs and the value of the product may not warrant the additional effort whereas the more expensive product may well need to be strictly controlled.

Other points where the accuracy of stock records are in jeopardy are at the point where the goods are received. The accurate receipt of product from the supplier at the warehouse needs to be well controlled as if, for example, the goods have the incorrect SKU ticket the receipt will automatically reflect against the wrong product in the scanning process. The withdrawal of stock from warehouse shelves and is subsequently picked and packed for store delivery has to be correctly recorded in order that the balances remain credible.

The receipt by the store is usually done at face value in order that the flow of goods to the sales floor is continuous. This heightens the possibility of pilferage in transit in spite of various preventative security measures. There is also the risk of incorrect documentation or suspect manipulation during the hand over processes.

Where disputes between the stores and the warehouse or distribution centre do arise the settlement of the claim tends to linger on as neither party wish to take on a negative mark against their shrinkage results with the result that final resolution often does not happen.

System errors or incorrect information is very real in the transmission of data between platforms which can go undetected until such stage that the all ills are blamed on "the system" which generates a mistrust which is not easily challenged or disproved but even worse, decisions and adjustments are made using incorrect data.

TECHNOLOGY

Up to now the focus has been on the planning and buying infrastructure required to procure product and ensure the efficiencies that will enable the maximization of the profit opportunities. However this will not be entirely possible unless the product is as close to perfect in terms of meeting predetermined quality standards, the addition of new or innovative features, is safe and meets the ever changing social and global needs. These are the factors or pillars that underpin the very reason for the existence of technology.

Quality

A product achieves a high standard of quality if it presents well on display, fits well, wears well, washes well, is fit for purpose, offers value for money, is free from any defects, insufficiencies and is unhampered from deviance to standards.

The activities need to ensure that the product meets the stated design, technical tolerances, fit, and fabric and colour specifications. This is often easier said than done. Supplier capabilities must be freely available to achieve this as well as the fact that unclear communications of expectations and standards may result in specifications not being met due to time and cost pressures.

Innovation

In order that the offering remains competitive it is imperative that new features or attributes are implemented constantly. For this to happen it requires the continual investment in new, improved ways of developing and producing product or materials. Innovation may be related to the fabric, components, treatments, end product attributes, packaging or sources of supply.

Inventive construction can add value the garment in terms of form and function such as adjustable waistbands for improved comfort. The secure lock stitching of buttons and other small items on children's garments which reduce the possibility of them being swallowed. The use of especially engineered interlinings which have more resilience enable garments to be totally machine washable, for example in the case of men's suits.

Social and environmental responsibilities

In the modern day and age most people are very aware of the responsibilities that suppliers are required to meet in order to keep the world as sustainable as possible.

The use of organic fabrics like cotton that is derived from organically grown crops, the unsavoury practice of child labour in production process, the structures in place for the removal of chemical wastes and many others are issues which are continually challenged.

The evolution of production units in China initially did not see environmental awareness as a primary focus as they were more concerned with survival but as they have developed, the treatment of waste and use of electricity has become a more important factor to be considered and the laying down of guidelines and regulations have become the norm. Although the Chinese have become environmentally sensitive and implement environment protection measures there is still the tendency to focus more on the protection of personal health. The situation is in the process of slowly improving to protect other environmental factors largely due to the improved education standards of younger management.

The key points of attention for sustainable environment awareness is the measurement and constantly improving efforts to reduce electricity consumption with the reduction of energy targets in place and the use of solar panel technology or even something as simple as the siting of administration desks next to windows. The same applies to the reduced use of water and where possible the practice to use recycled water has been introduced.

Safety

The safety of the customer must always be paramount as there are volumes of examples of where people have been injured or worse due to unsafe or defective product. Technology should constantly strive to meet the highest standards of safety in their products as well as that of the plants in which they are manufactured and the logistical process that is followed in order to get the product to market. Where required, the customer should be fully informed of particular risks inherent to the products.

If supplier's products do not conform to safety regulations they are subject to risks particularly where the required certificates are not available to show that they have met the obligatory regulations. The standards should be documented on laboratory test reports and supported by the pre-production samples either completed by the retailer's technologists or an accredited independent third party external laboratory. In some of the large trusted suppliers there may be internal specialists who self-regulate this process but this may present a challenge where there is a broad range of product categories being manufactured.

Fabric Technology

In the buying arena an integral part of the role is a pre requisite knowledge of textiles and the beginning to end production process associated with garment creation. With a good understanding of fabrics the product appeal, value and innovation aspects can be maximised and the most appropriate material can be identified for a product that will deliver the required performance to best meet the end user requirements and expectations. The briefing and negotiating process with suppliers is also able to be conducted with greater authority and credibility.

Ongoing development of new fabrics is reliant on inputs from various sources such as that of designers, buyers, suppliers, mills, yarn providers as well as the dyestuff and chemical suppliers. A healthy interaction between the main players permit the fabric innovation decisions to be made earlier and consequentially enable quicker product development.

The production process using fibres converted to yarns together with processing through to the finished product can be outlined as follows

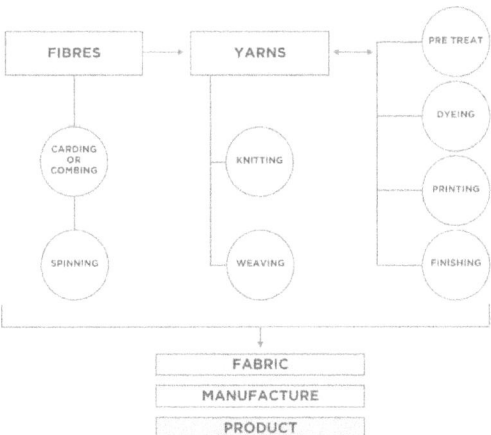

Fibres

The essential requirements for fibres to be spun into yarns is that it must be at least five millimetres in length and should be flexible and strong enough. Other inherent properties should include elasticity, fineness, uniformness, durability and a measure of lustre.

Fibres are either natural which tend to be predisposed to irregularities or synthetic that are more consistent and easier to control. Through the blending of both types in varying proportions it is possible to achieve a bit of the best of both worlds.

The continual developments of new and blends of fibres have transformed the performance of many fabrics particularly in terms of the form, function, safety and fashionability. Typical examples of this is the reduction of creasing and the evolvement of easy care properties.

Staple fibres which are of defined lengths are used for the construction of both natural and synthetic yarns whereas man-made filament fibres are extruded from natural gases and oil and stretched into continuous strands to manufacture synthetic yarns.

The properties of fibres vary dependent on the source. Natural fibres such as cotton absorb moisture well but need to be well prepared to counteract shrinkage, stretching, fading or being eaten by fish moths. Synthetic polyester has good easy to care properties, does not shrink or stretch and is economical but is not very absorbent. A blended combination of yarns from natural and synthetic parents take on the characteristics of both and the extent to which this is achieved is dependent on the combined proportions.

Yarns

Yarn is a continuous length of twisted or interlocked fibres which are used in the production of textiles, crocheting, knitting, weaving, embroidery, and rope making. There are two types being staple yarns that are spun from natural fibres and filament yarns which are derived from synthetic fibres.

Spinning of yarns may be of the same fibre or can be a blend of natural and synthetic fibres in varying proportions. The properties of warmth, lightness, durability or softness of handle can be achieved to a higher or lesser degree through the varying of the ratios in the blending in order to best utilise the positive characteristics of each fibre. An example is the polyester and cotton blend where the original cotton characteristics of softness and breathability are retained whilst the polyester offers the strength, wrinkle and mildew resistance.

Cotton yarns can either be combed whereby during the process a stronger and more luxurious yarn is created and the hairy surplus of the fibre is removed in comparison to carded yarns which have less body and are more hairy.

Yarn counts

Yarn count is a numerical measurement of the fineness of the yarn that denotes the relationship of the weight and length of yarn. As a rule, the finer the count, the more expensive is the fabric and it will be lighter if compared to like constructions with subjectively nicer handle and drape.

Sewing threads

Sewing threads are special kinds of yarn that are engineered and designed to pass rapidly through a sewing machine needle to efficiently form a stitch and to function without breaking for the life of a sewn product. The most commonly used fine fibres are cotton, nylon, polyester and rayon.

Fabric

Fabric is a flexible two dimensional material that consists of a network of natural or artificial fibres which are suitable for use in the production of clothes. The formation of the fabric is constructed through the interlacing of yarns known as weaving or in the case of knitting, it is the interloping of yarns.

Fabric weight

The standard global measurement of fabric weight is grams per square metre (gsm). Factors that can influence the weight is the combination of yarns, yarn counts, knitting gauges, weaves and any finishes that are applied.

Knitted fabrics

Knitting is where the raw materials in the form of yarn are knitted into unfinished material commonly known as greige fabric. This is done by the use of needles that intermesh the yarn into loops. The weight of the fabric will be dependent of the yarn count as well as the gauge of the yarn. The foremost types of knitted fabrics are single jersey, ribs, interlock and fleece.

The machines that knit can either be circular or flat in setup. Circular machines do weft knitting which is where the yarns run horizontally across the width the fabric with the needles moving either collectively or individually to form loops. Flat knitting machines do warp knitting where the yarns run vertically through the length of the fabric and all the needles are used collectively to form the loops.

Single Jersey fabrics

The common construction of single jersey fabrics is 24-28 gauge and have a weight of approximately 120-200gsm. Single jersey is mostly used for products such as t-shirts, sleepwear, leggings and bedding.

The advantage is that it can be blended with other fabrics, such as elastane, has comfort as well as stretch, drapes well and is great value. The downsides are that it is prone to shrinkage and if blended with polyester it is likely to pill and have less absorbency.

Rib fabrics

The feature of ribbed fabric is that it displays plain and purl stitches along the course on both sides of the fabric and consists of alternating raised and depressed wales.

The characteristics of rib fabrics are that it offers better fit support, is warm as it traps air in the structure and drapes better than woven fabrics. However the finished fabric is generally more expensive than single jersey, has higher shrinkage than woven and because of the ridge structure it is difficult to print on. The finishing of the cuffs and waist bands need to be combined with elastane to function effectively. The fabric is commonly used for t-shirts and styled tops.

Interlock fabrics

Interlock fabrics are knitted on circular machines and the structure looks the same on the back and front of the fabric. It is a typical winter fabric and is commonly used for tracksuits and sleepwear.

The pros of interlock is that it is warmer than single jersey and is also heavier which gives it better thermal properties. It can be combined with viloft or Lycra and has better drape than woven material. The cons are that it shrinks more than woven, is unstable during processing and has poor recovery which is illustrated for example where garments may bag at the knees or stretch inconsistently.

Warp knits versus weft knits

Warp knits offer better stability with less shrinkage than wefts and commonly use synthetic yarns. They have a vertical stripe and are commonly used for swimwear, lace, mesh and net material.

Weft knits are used more often with natural fibres and have more stretch than warp knits. Stripes are horizontal and more often than not are used for t-shirts, fleece, underwear, sleepwear or tights.

Generally knitted garments are predominantly more casual, comfortable to wear and always stretchy, easy to wash, often wrinkle free and relatively inexpensive. Unfortunately they lack crispness and are not as dressy as woven, can shrink, stretch and lose shape and therefore can quickly look shabby and unflattering.

Woven fabrics

There are two main types of woven fabrics, namely plain or twill. Other woven fabrics include satins, sateen, dobby and jacquards.

Plain weave is the most basic woven fabric where the warp and the weft are so aligned that they form a simple crisscross pattern such as in poplin, shirting and canvas where the thickness of the yarn determines the characteristic of the fabric. Plain weaves are mostly seen in shirts, shorts, sheeting and tablecloths.

While they are more affordable than other weaves and are generally more stable than knits but there can be a tendency for seam slippage or poor tear strength with lighter weights.

The twill weave differs to the plain weave in that the weft thread passes over one or more warp threads and then under one or more and so on. This type of weave is commonly used for chino trousers, denims, jackets, curtains and cushions.

Twill weaves have a defined face and more drape than plain weaves but are more prone to seam slippage.

Overall woven fabrics appear crisper, are smarter, look pristine and seldom shrink or lose shape. They are, however, relatively more expensive than knits, not as soft and do not stretch which can make the garment feel restrictive in terms of comfort. Washing is more arduous or requires dry cleaning and the fabric wrinkles more easily.

While the warp yarns run lengthwise in the fabric and the weft yarns run across the width the fabric the fabric also has a face and a back with the face side having a better appearance which usually forms the outside of the garment.

PRODUCTION

During production it is important that the most suitable fabric is utilised to ensure the best performance of the product for the intended end use. What is equally significant is the specifications of all the components, make up and fit criteria and that benchmark quality tolerances or allowances are set to safeguard that the product meets all the form and function requirements. The responsibility for this aspect lies with garment technology and quality control.

Manufacturing Plant

An example of a typical factory layout can be illustrated as follows which facilitates the free flow of material and operations in a structured way that alleviates the risk of congestion or bottle necks.

A simple example of the factory layout and flow

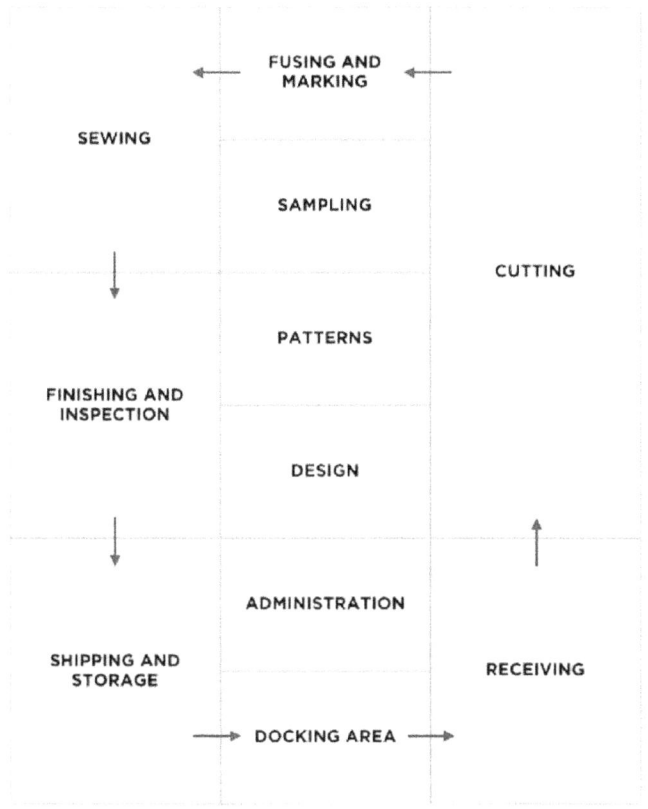

Manufacturing process

The process that is followed in the manufacture of a garment from beginning to end can be depicted as follows which is accommodated by the free flow factory design.

Drawing or sketch
An image of the concept for the garment is prepared to assist the pattern maker in understanding the style details required when constructing the patterns.

Basic block
A standard block with correct proportions is outlined by the pattern maker which is then used to construct a working pattern to be utilised by the sewing unit.

Working pattern
Sample machinists require a base to create a garment which is presented in the form of a working pattern and may or may not be modified during the sampling process.

Sample making
The concept or representative idea is created from a working pattern to be assembled into garment form. This may not necessarily be done using the intended fabric in order to save costs but are primarily used to analyse the pattern fit and design. The sample is then reviewed by a panel of designers, pattern makers and sewing specialists who can recommend changes.

Costing
The fundamental cost structure is determined based on the fabric usage and the time taken to produce the garment known as the labour minute rating.

Production pattern

The final perfect pattern evolves from the working pattern and is used in bulk production. There are various tolerances and allowances that are accommodated for during the pattern make. Examples may be the over body tolerance which is built into the fit of the garment to allow ease of movement within the size parameters, a shrinkage allowance which is added to the pattern piece in the width and the length accommodates fabric shrinkage during printing.

Grading

The provision for the size spread is done by a pattern grader who creates patterns in different sizes by scaling the sample size, which is usually a middle size production pattern up or down. This may be done manually or by a computer. Production samples of the graded pattern samples are made and tested for fit and serve as a point of reference.

Marker making

Patterns are developed from standard blocks or measurement charts. An advantage of basic blocks is that there is a consistent reference which ensures that the sizing is similar across different styles. The marker serves as a common base for pattern makers to work from thus allowing armhole balances to be correct, shoulder slopes to be the same across styles and ensure that a consistent minimum over body tolerance is in place.

Markers or the cutting plan are printed or drawn as an outline of the pattern parts onto paper that is the same width and length of the fabric which is positioned on top of the lay and held in place by weights. This is an essential step in the manufacture process as it serves as a guide for the operator during the cutting procedure.

The rating or consumption is the actual amount of fabric required to cut a specific garment and the adequacy of a marker is the percentage of the fabric that is covered by the cut patterns. The less unused fabric which is not covered by the patterns, the higher is the efficiency as it should be remembered that the waste is still included in the cost of the garment. Other factors that influence the efficiency of fabric usage is different pile directions or one way characteristics, stripes or checks that need to match, border prints, size ratios and the number of units.

As with grading this operation can be done manually or by using computer software packages which make the task less cumbersome.

Fabric spread
In order to prepare for the cutting process the fabric is spread out on tables. The extent of the lay will be calculated according to the marker and the number of lays which determines the lay height to meet the order plan of a specific contract.

Cutting
The most common cutting process is done using a powered cutting machine suitable for the type of cloth. As technology has progressed in the modern age the cutting operation driven by computerized programmes have become more popular.

The height of the lay should be such that it allows the easy manoeuvring of straight blades through the lay and preventing the possibility for the lay to shift in spite of weights being used to keep the paper markers in place. Band knife machines are used to cut smaller panels such as cuffs and collars.

Fusing is used commonly for collars, cuffs, facings, garment panels and waistbands utilising a machine that applies heat and pressure for the operation.

Where products need to be processed, for example garment washing, the quantities are set up in smaller lays to enable completed garments to be sent to the processor in manageable quantities.

Bundling

It is important that dye lots are be separated to avoid colour variations on panels when garments are sewn and therefore the cut panels are sorted into complete garments by size and separate dye lots. The grouping of these cut sections are numbered and then bundled ready to be sent to the sewing section.

Sewing

After the sorted bundles are received they can be stitched. For example, the sleeves, bodice and collars are assembled and stitched together to complete the final form of the garment.

It is important that certain elements are compatible with the fabric such as the stich type, machine and needle type, seam and thread widths, all of which will be contribute towards the appearance, functionality and cost of the garment.

The most common stitch types are:

Lock stitch which is used mainly in visible areas such as top stitching and on collars as well as for the insertion of zips.

Over locking stitches are utilised to cover raw edges of exposed seams.

Safety stitches which are predominantly used for the joining seams mostly for woven and denim fabrics.

Mock safety stitches are also used for the joining of seams but mainly for knitted fabrics.

Chain stitch close seams of mainly woven and denim products.

Cover stitch is used in the main in undergarments to conceal elastics or to cover hems and can also serve as a decorative feature.

Blind stitches generally close hems on garments such as trousers or skirts.

Seams

The characteristics of a seam that is well constructed is that they are strong, durable, have a good relative elasticity, are secure and neat.

The performance of the seam will be influenced the weight, strength and durability of the fabric together with the seam construction, stitches per centimetre, strength and elasticity of thread used.

Specialised seaming such as darts, pleats, tucks, binding and piping as well as gauging require higher levels of operator skills.

The most common seam types are:

Plain seams are the simplest and used most often in various products from pillows to pants.

French seams have a clean finished look and are used successfully on high slippage fabrics which are susceptible to fraying and are also used with sheer materials to conceal the thread. Such seams are commonly employed on fabrics such as satin, sateen, voile and organza types.

Lap or posted seams are used typically on bulky fabrics that do not ravel like leathers, felt and denim.

Bound seams provide a cleaner finish and aesthetic appeal on mainly light weight fabrics more often for silk or linings of jackets.

Blind seams deliver a neat appearance and prevent rough edges for products as in lined drapes, curtains, blinds and denim side seams.

Ironing and finishing

After the sewing process is complete the final stage of finishing can take place which may include some form of decoration like that of the stitching of a cuff, the addition of a pocket or emblems, buttons or velcro snap fasteners.

As collars are a focal point of the garment they will always require special attention. Precise cutting of the fabrics and interlinings, the fusing conditions and perfect profile stitching is essential for good quality balanced appearances.

In order to be functional, pockets must be of an adequate width, depth and strength. Mitred corners need to be of equal length and balanced especially where the pocket is a styling feature. It is important therefore that the position is correct, that the shape is precise and the sewing detail is perfect.

Due to the nature of processed garments stricter controls are required to achieve the best end result. Particular attention needs to be given to thread selection which has to be stronger, the selection of fusing and wadding in jackets must be such that it will not delaminate or disintegrate and fabric shrinkage needs to be closely monitored so that the garment does not become distorted.

The garment needs to be made neat and tidy through the removal of loose threads, fibre and fluff. Final checks are done which include the detection of needles for obvious safety reasons.

Pressing is an essential part of the garment presentation. The methods and equipment will be dependent on product and fabric type in order to achieve the desired garment appeal.

The finished garment is sent to the packing section where it is ticketed, labelled and packaged.

Inspection

Inspection of the product is done during the production process at each critical key point and the type of defects that are watched out for are open seams, incorrect stitching techniques, non-matching threads or improper creasing.

After production is complete the detection of defects is repeated but attention is also given to any possible colour mismatches, incorrect sizing of components, missing buttons and inappropriate trimmings.

Audits of quality standards take place at various stages and places to make sure that the best possible product is delivered. The audit process starts with the pre-production sample where all stakeholders agree on the standards that must be met to set the established benchmarks to which the end of line garments will be compared. Tolerances are set up front such as the percentage defects that will be accepted before a declaration of failure for each category of imperfections. Such declared tolerances will avoid future disputes in the event of whether or not a garment with defects qualifies as a reject.

Roving in line inspections also take place at various points during production for both measurement and construction to ensure the set criteria is being met.

A zero defect would be where the imperfection could be a safety risk to the consumer like insecure studs or protruding metal ribbing in corsetry.

A serious defect is such that the consequence would result in product failure or render the product to be unsaleable as in the case of broken stitches, excessive grinning and holes.

Minor defects are classified where the product would still be useable but does not meet the acceptable standards like loose threads that could result in reduced sales.

Other options of random testing may exist at picking and packing stage by either the retailer's representatives or an authorized agent.

It is important that a system is in place whereby it is ensured that reject garments are isolated, labels removed and clearly marked in order that they do not get included again with passed garments. The rate of rejects should be measured and analysed as an endeavour to minimise the failure rate.

Packing
The packing of the product is done according to specified techniques possibly using templates in such a way to ensure that the quality and integrity of the garment is maintained.

Cartons
Placing product into cartons is the final packing operation of the garment prior to shipment. The quantity per carton and the configuration within must be consistent. The labelling and markings on the carton has to be as per the regulatory requirements and as part of the quality check there should be a reconciliation of what the contents should be and what they actually are.

Production systems
The variety of configurations of the layout of sewing machine production lines can be set out in several ways and the selection of the most appropriate arrangement will be determined by the nature and quantity of product being manufactured.

Possible optional configurations for a production line

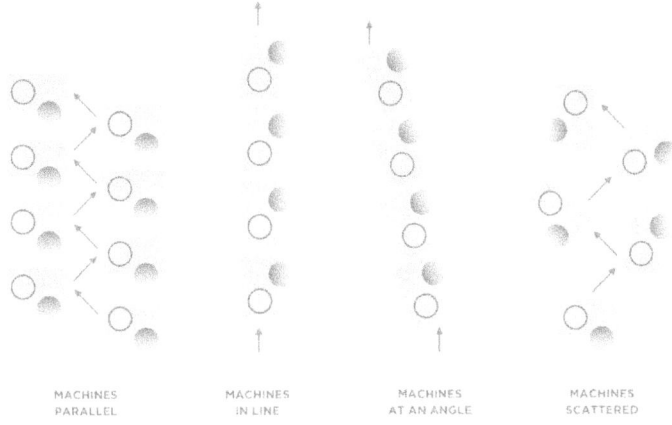

| MACHINES PARALLEL | MACHINES IN LINE | MACHINES AT AN ANGLE | MACHINES SCATTERED |

In the main the appropriate production system is set up based on the product style, types of machines and availability of the required operator skill level.

The layout of the equipment will also vary dependent on the nature of the product type in the factory and the system employed may well include the smooth integration of the material handling, production process and the personnel that will direct the workflow to deliver the finished product.

One of the typical production systems that is generally used is the make through system where one operator will do all the stages of the sewing operation from beginning to end and after completion will commence with the next garment. Although this is easy to supervise it delivers a comparatively low productivity and is dependent on highly experienced operators and therefore comes with a high labour cost. This type of format is suited to the manufacture of couture garments and sample making.

The modular system of production is where an organised group of individuals work together to accomplish a common purpose and the layout is sequential in a parallel formation where each operator is assigned at least one task adjacent to each other.

The detail operations at each station, for example in the manufacture of a t-shirt at each key point needs to be carefully planned to ensure maximum operational and time efficiency.

Example of detailed operation at each station for the manufacture of a t-shirt

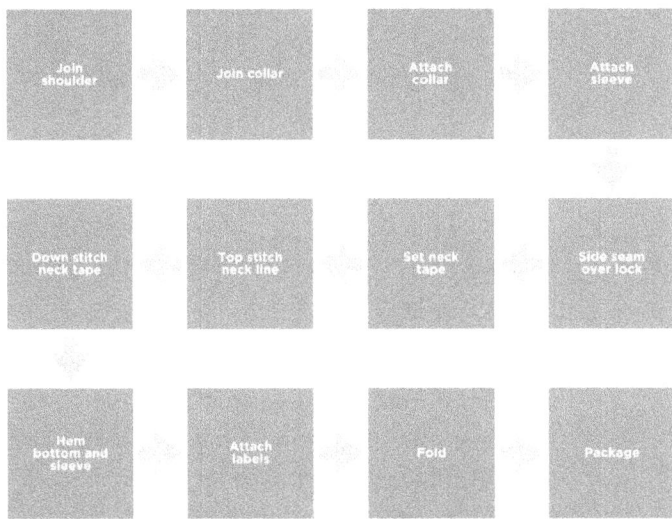

The flow will naturally influence the selection of the production line configuration and in all likelihood the t-shirt will possibly follow the path as illustrated in the first figure above.

An assembly line system is where each operator is assigned a task and the bundles are moved down the line sequentially to complete each task as is illustrated in the second and third configuration options.

A system of unit production is where a few styles can be mass produced and may be manufactured at the same time. The operator completes the production of one piece of the garment and then moves it onto the next operator so there are single garments being passed from one operator to the next as a single unit and is not in bundles. The work stations are positioned closely together in order to minimise the amount of the movement required to grasp the component from the carrier that continually moves between the work stations as is illustrated in the last figure.

Quick response manufacturing

More and more suppliers are placing emphasis on achieving the benefits of higher quality and speed in the production cycle where they may be manufacturing in lesser or varying volumes.

This objective is assisted by the choice of suitable production process configurations with the correct machinery and right attachments such as folders. The needle and thread types should be such that they enable the efficient manufacture of the product type.

The advantage of quick response manufacturing is that it increases machine up time and therefore delivers an improved quality and subsequently less rework. Where this process is linked to a team incentive programme a consequence is lower staff turnover with fewer social noncompliance issues while also empowering employees.

Typical quick response initiatives is to have product stored at various stages of production so that it is possible to react swiftly to current consumer sales patterns. A prime example is where garments such as knitwear, sweaters, t-shirts, tank tops and the like are made up in uncoloured greige yarn and as the demand happens the garments are then piece dyed to whatever colours the market calls for. Not only in such cases is the benefit of improved sales achieved but it also reduces the build-up of unwanted garments or yarns. Other tactics include the reservation of production capacity but holding back the ordering of fabric and finalisation of the style for as long as possible in order to react more closely to trends as quickly as possible.

Through these actions the retailer is able to better serve their customer in a faster time which increases their competitiveness and offers the opportunity of potential growth in market share.

PACKAGING TECHNOLOGY

The packaging of a product is largely the responsibility of a packaging technologist and plays a critical role in the presentation, protection and communication of information to the consumer as well as taking into account the ecological demands of the environment.

The common purpose of packaging is that it physically protects the product against mechanical shocks, vibrations, varying temperatures, humidity and excessive handling during transit or warehousing. The usual provision of information whether it is on the packaging itself or through the use of labels, indicate any regulations that may apply, the usage and safety instructions, transport guidelines and lists the components and chemicals that were used in the production process.

Packaging assists in the sale of the product in that it serves as a "silent salesman". There is a communication of information through clever graphic design that encompasses the properties of the product, instructions as how to use the merchandise and the provision of safety warnings. Convenience is added by way of easy storage configurations, display conformity and the accommodation of barcoding information which is easily accessible for scanners to capture sales and stock keeping records and store them on a common data base.

Specialised packaging plays an important part in securing the product through the use of tamper proof mechanisms and can also be engineered to reduce the pilferage.

Over packaging should be avoided and where possible the utilisation of recycled or recyclable materials in the manufacturing process is encouraged without affecting the functional properties.

Outer cartons must adhere to weight and dimension stipulations and should be able to be easily handled on warehouse equipment such as conveyer belts, pallets and storage slots.

Of the two types, primary packaging enjoys the journey of the product right to the end user while secondary packaging is that which is discarded at various points during the journey.

Examples of primary packaging are self- adhesive tickets which carry the barcode detail, price, reference numbers, colour and size as well as date codes. Swing tickets are used where adhesive tickets are not appropriate and may also be independently attached in order to highlight any unique features of the product. Invariably adhesive tickets are applied to presentation packs, wallets and plastic bags.

Sew in labels are typically a satin tape which is sewn into the garment side or neck seam and carry wash care instructions, product reference numbers, size information, fabric composition, country of origin as well as safety instructions. The fibre content must be described by its generic name but may be accompanied by a brand name or a trade mark. An example would be where woollen products will display the wool mark for which the supplier will have qualified to utilise through their manufacturing process.

An example of garment care and reference label

EXAMPLE OF A GARMENT CARE AND REFERENCE LABEL

Care markings are not legally required but are commonly indicated by the universal symbols that are consistent and accurate, for example, where a garment needs to be hand washed only and not machine washed it will be highlighted using the relevant symbol

Universal care instruction symbols are key to the garment label and the most common are outlined below

Symbol	Description	Symbol	Description
[60°]	WASHING WATER TEMPERATURE	⊠	DO NOT TUMBLE DRY
(hand wash)	HAND WASH ONLY	⊘	DRIP DRY IN SHADE
(wash)	WASH ON SENSITIVE PROGRAMMES	[|||]	DRIP DRY
⊠	DO NOT WASH	[−]	DRY FLAT
(P)	DRY CLEANABLE	⊓	DRY ON HANGER
⊗	DO NOT DRY CLEAN	⊠	DO NOT IRON
⊠ (bleach)	DO NOT USE BLEACH	(iron ·)	IRON WITH WARM IRON
⊠	DO NOT TUMBLE DRY	(iron ···)	IRON WITH HOT IRON

Country of origin is displayed on labels to indicate geographically where the significant stage of production took place. In most countries this is a legal requirement even if the garment may have some components that originate from other parts of the world. Apart from it being law, the identification gives the consumer the choice of which countries that they may wish to support or not support for political or emotional reasons and participate in buy local promotional campaigns that are designed to stimulate local employment.

Swing tags that describe features or unique properties of products have to be truthful in terms of fit for purpose and of the quality standard that is expected by the customer. Where the product does not meet these claims they can be deemed to be misleading and could have legal implications that can be enforced either by the user or competitors who may feel unfairly disadvantaged. An example of this could be that where a ticket describes the garment as being non-iron but after a few washes it has to be ironed.

Secondary packaging are items such as outer cartons, over bags for hanging product, hanger size indicators, stock room and store address labels, the outer carton product detail and supplier detail stamps.

The procuring and specifying of ecologically friendly packaging should always be done keeping the safety of the environs top of mind. Printing should be done keeping volatile compound emissions to a minimum through, for example, the use of vegetable based ink that are free from heavy metals.

Measures need to be put in place to keep waste of inks, ink tins, and paper to a minimum and the cleaning and recirculation of polluted water should be promoted. Paper packaging and corrugated cartons ought to contain a percentage of recycled papers and must not to have been bleached using chlorine. Plastic packaging should be of recyclable materials such as polypropylene and polyethylene.

SUPPLIERS

Sourcing suppliers

The assessment of a prospective supplier or vendor, mill, dye house, fibre producer, processor, trimming and component contractor, packaging supplier and printer is a process that needs to be done thoroughly in order to ensure that they meet all the required criteria to manufacture the product in mind.

In principle there are four different methodologies of purchasing product.

The majority of garment purchases conducted by the retailer is as per the processes described in this book which is conceived based on inputs from the design, buying, merchandising and technical teams whereby the criteria of fabric, components, style and manufacturing as well as the packaging are dictated to the supplier.

Secondly, as is practiced by the more traditional retailers is where they buy their own fabric and allocate it out to a cut, make and trim supplier. The supplier may or may not offer a style, which could be provided by the retailer to a number of different suppliers to obtain a quote for the manufacture of the product according to a labour minute rating. The price of the fabric is static as it is supplied by the retailer. The downside of this methodology is that the retailer must have a technical understanding of fabrics which means that the buying team needs to be more knowledgeable and have added skills which are not always readily available in the labour market. There is also the need to invest in fabric stocks and have a detailed understanding of minute rates or manufacturing costs of the supplier. On the plus side of cut, make and trim manufacturing is that it enables the ability to cost accurately, be more flexible in selection of styling and achieve a greater speed to market.

A third methodology of sourcing is the direct purchase of a completed ready designed garment from the supplier where the retailer's brand label is inserted and the style is procured exclusively for the retailer.

Lastly there is the option to procure popular brands directly out of the supplier's range. In this case it is likely that there will be no flexibility in terms of modifying the style and often the investment of building a store within a store concept may be required. Pricing tends to be at a premium and commonly minimum order quantities apply.

The researching of new, cheaper, innovative and exciting sources of supply in order to maintain a competitive advantage in the market place is an ongoing process, as is the need to maintain a sustainable relationship with current core suppliers which comes with a continual effort to improve their delivery standards of product. Suppliers are expected to be consistently reliable, effective and efficient to retain the business of their clients as the success of the retailers is the guarantee of continued acceptance of the product that they produce.

A constant balance of those products which are sourced from local suppliers and that which are manufactured off shore is important. As off shore suppliers improve in terms of quality, equipment and workforce living standards there is an increasing pressure on costs and therefore the sources do not remain geographically static.

Fashion buying was originally focused in the Far East in Hong Kong and Taiwan but costs are increasing faster than they have in the past as well as pressure is being placed on authorities to elevate minimum wage bands. It is therefore not surprising that production is moving to more cost efficient areas such as Indonesia, Bangladesh, Pakistan, Cambodia, and Vietnam while production in Madagascar and Mauritius has also become prevalent.

Hong Kong and Taiwan have now become more the management and design centres who procure from alternative production plants. The ease of increased technology, the relaxing of bureaucratic barriers as well as cheaper travel has enabled the transfer of production to be relatively easy and flexible. Migration of production to newer countries brings limitations and therefore it is important to maximise efficiencies in the current countries where goods are produced while at the same time sourcing alternative manufacturing plants that will meet the ethical and quality standards of the retailer.

Added to this is the probability that the larger the offshore supplier is, the more the likelihood is that the retailer will be less important in their lives and if need be, the order can be more easily forfeited. The converse is that if the overseas supplier is small the possibility exists that the production may be outsourced to other vendors who the retailer may not even know about. Overseas factories seldom readily have excess production capacity and that this together with the longer transport lead times make the possibility of repeat orders within the same season improbable.

Sourcing internationally does, at face value, often appear to be very attractive but there are factors that need to be taken into account which can lead to additional unforeseen costs as well as logistical challenges particularly in terms of lead times. The re-organisation of production can therefore be perplexing and the savings that may be apparent up front could indeed be decimated later down the line.

Keeping track of the off shore supply chain at times presents some complex challenges and makes it very difficult to monitor the progress of product at all times. An extreme illustration of such a scenario is where the process commences with the raw material producer who passes the product onto the commodities traders whose purchasing agents sells them onto the garment manufacturers. In the procedure local distributors could be involved to deliver the raw materials to the garment manufacturing plant. Secondary vendors for outsourced processes are frequently utilised before the product is delivered eventually to the local exporters and freighters administered by agents on behalf of the larger trading houses who are the frontline liaison with the retailer.

Advantages may be enjoyed by having a dedicated foreign office in key cities to control the management of suppliers and product. Obviously this does come at an added cost and should only be considered when a critical mass in that foreign country is achieved. However, the formation of such an organisation must be assessed on merit as to whether it is viable or not. Typically such a team will consist of two or three merchandisers, possibly buying and sourcing specialists together with maybe three or four quality controllers who spend two to three days a week in the factories focusing exclusively on the retailer's orders. The foreign office owns the relationship with the supplier and are able to exert pressure to ensure critical deadlines are met. Communication is easier and faster as such teams are self-managed and can be flexible in evaluating priorities.

The extreme example of the complexity of dealing with offshore suppliers is that of the world's largest trading house being the Hong Kong based sourcing and logistical company, Li Fung. They own no factories or mills but simply play matchmaker between poor countries factories and vendors which have favourable labour rates and costs and the global retailers for whom Li Fung handle the logistics.

Li Fung represent some fifteen thousand suppliers across sixty countries which enable them to procure very high volumes and have them produced in a fraction of a time that a single supplier would take to complete. It is not surprising that consequently they are known as the "Walmart of purchasing" and the sheer size of the organisation makes it difficult to pin point the true sources of the product and they have been alleged from time to time to be linked to several calamities in some dubious factories.

Where the retailer is dominant in their target market and the volumes are substantial enough it is advantageous for them to cut out the middleman agent and procure directly from the source. By doing this an advantage is gained over their competitors and they do not end up subsidising the supply chain for their rivals especially where full containers are bought on a repeat basis. Advantage is also to be gained through using a buying agent or consolidator to combine the products into full container loads where they purchase from multiple off shore suppliers.

Currency exchange rate fluctuations may well change the advantage of buying off shore, as will quota limitations which could change in the exporting country due to the fact that costs will probably increase should the availability of the quotas become scarcer.

The management of offshore deliveries is more complex and if minimum order quantities are imposed they can lead to higher storage costs and inventory investment together with varying transport charges.

The intricate nature of international freight forwarding requires either an in house dedicated team or the need to outsource this function to an agency to take on the responsibility.

Often the additional travelling and increased management costs are not taken into account when considering product quotations. The opening of foreign offices with sourcing, quality control and buying teams in itself can be a considerable additional overhead that needs to be established, staffed and equipped and is excluded from the base garment cost.

Frequently the bulk offshore deliveries have to be unpacked and repacked and labelled after allocation that results in multiple handling which adds considerable cost and time delay.

For the reasons above the viability of sourcing from foreign suppliers has to be carefully considered in terms of the minimum volumes that need to be procured to achieve the benefits while at the same time being able to exceed the sales potential without putting strain on the warehouse storage capabilities.

It is therefore strategically beneficial if the supply chain from overseas is as short as possible with the minimum of cross over proprietorship points, for example, the allocation of product while it is in transit lessens the pressure of receiving and warehousing of the goods before being withdrawn for picking and packing. The possibility exists that the goods can bypass the storage stage and be delivered directly to the pick pack areas of the distribution centre. This type of approach might be appropriate for one off promotions and special events.

The advantages of a local supplier base is quicker potential delivery to market, more flexible production with easily manageable inventory quantities and less complicated administration, quality control and payment methodologies. For local suppliers the trend has also shifted towards smaller production infrastructures with specialisation on exclusivity and individualistic styling.

The relationship between retailers and local suppliers is most often one of mutual interdependence all of which has to be weighed up against the cost and innovation advantages of off shore suppliers. The manufacture of replenishment core type product is better suited to local manufacturers as it calls for the fine-tuning of styles, colour and size ratios which are easier to adjust. There may also be pressure from the authorities to encourage local production through the various "Buy Local" promotions in order to stimulate the local industry and satisfy the employment initiatives in the political arena.

It stands to reason that the less suppliers there are, the less the burden of supplier management will be with regard to different administration models, quality control and varying costs.

A strategy to rationalise suppliers eliminates smaller, incompatible, problematic suppliers who are often more demanding in terms of the time required to manage them compared to the effort spent on more substantial, streamlined producers and enable effective performance management.

The larger the quantities allocated to fewer suppliers will lead to lower cost prices through the economies of scale advantage as well as the benefit of the delivery of improved quality and reliability. Management communication and the mutual interdependence with specialised service provision will undoubtedly lead to a competitive advantage.

There are however risks involved in dealing with too few suppliers in that the exposure to greater innovation is limited and complacent suppliers tend to offer more and more of the same or wait for the retailer to provide ideas and designs. Often the production methods are inflexible which could result in a relationship of mistrust and frustration.

Newer suppliers can be added to the core base of suppliers, however, the number of suppliers in total should remain constant through the consistent measurement of performance including formal review processes being in place for existing suppliers. If they do not meet the performance criteria they run the risk of elimination.

The performance review and assessment of suppliers should not be done in isolation by each department that they supply but preferably conducted across the business as a whole which will deliver more objective and consistent results and thereby will avoid mixed messages being given to suppliers.

Other pitfalls that retailers need to be aware of is the differing perceptions of the suppliers versus that of the buyers. Typically buyers view suppliers as being frequently older and more experienced, full of excuses and promise the world. From the suppliers point of view the buyers are young and inexperienced, abuse their buying power and utilise threats to make unrealistic demands and apart from being busy all the time, the formation of a sustainable relationship is disrupted due to the regular changing of staffing in departments.

It is not uncommon that buyers and designers tend to make last minute changes to designs, trims, quantities and colours which puts immense pressure on suppliers and consequently leads to the need to work excessive overtime hours or over book production capacity. As a result they may end up using unqualified outside vendors in an effort to accommodate the revised unreasonable deadlines and can thereby easily transgress the compliance criteria.

Conscious efforts are essential to influence the relationship to be one of joint co-operation and respect, the conducting of informed cost price negotiations with better transparency with regard to each other's needs and the working together to achieve solutions that will be for their mutual benefit.

There are some key questions that need to be answered before embarking on a relationship with a potential supplier which are:

What are the supplier's capabilities and specific skills?

Do they have design facilities and what level of innovation is evident?

Do they have the capacity requirements to meet the required volumes?

Is the planning of production stable in that it minimises changeovers and keeps labour fully utilised so that orders are not shifted around dependent on which customer is shouting the loudest.

Are they financially stable? Do they meet the criteria that ensures payment to their raw material suppliers being secure and guaranteed?

Do they have the appropriate equipment to deliver the envisioned product?

Is the production sub contracted to other vendors and do these producers also meet the same required compliance standards?

What are the initial costing indications in comparison to alternative sources?

Which other major retailers do they supply?

What management and liaison structures are in place?

What are their quality standards like and do they have current valid compliance audits from an accredited recognised test house?

Do they have the ability to produce or source in smaller batches to maximise flexibility and speed?

How close are they to their component suppliers?

Where are they located and will that have any bearing on meeting the delivery lead times, delivery demand schedules and costs?

Do they have any long term strategic expansion plans?

Does the physical building structure meet all building specifications, safety requirements and provide the appropriate facilities to accommodate a production environment?

Is there evidence that they are ethically compliant in terms of staff hours of work, remuneration policies and adherence to accepted norms of terms of employment?

Do they meet the environmental requirements in terms of health and safety of the workers?

Do they utilise any banned substances in the production process and what is the policy for the safe disposal of waste effluent?

Are the raw material suppliers reputable and certified?

What are their laboratory facilities or which testing facilities do they use?

The format of these initial audits can be formalized in a matrix form and scorecard values can be weighted according to the level of importance that can be depicted through a relative score compared to other suppliers which ensures a more objective assessment and structured plans of action for suppler selection.

A simple example of such a supplier rating matrix is as follows

	QUALITY	CAPACITY	GROWTH	COSTING	ENVIRON-MENT	SOCIAL	INNO-VATION	LIAISON	TOT	WEIGHTED AVERAGE
WEIGHTED IMPORTANCE	6	6	5	7	5	5	5	6		
SUPPLIER A	20	15	25	30	15	15	10	20	150	108
SUPPLIER B	25	20	30	25	20	20	25	10	175	123
SUPPLIER C	30	30	10	25	20	20	30	20	185	132

Key areas of compliance focus in the drafting of an audit report

Social compliance refers in the main as to how the company treats its employees and their perspective on social responsibility. The point of reference is to a minimal code of conduct that directs how employees are treated with regards to wages, working hours, work conditions, safety signage and preventitive measures such as lighting, electrical wiring and use of face masks, recruitment criteria, human resource policies in terms of disputes and promotions. What is absolutely essential is that they adhere to a set code of ethics to meet the compliance requirements.

Environmental compliance speaks to the respect that they have for environmental aspects such as the use of chemicals that may harm employees, disposal of waste products, pollution of water sources and the utisation of environmental enhancing components such as the use of organic cottons. Compliance audits ensure that they meet the minimum standards of various environmental laws.

Capabilities refers to the standards of vendors and their sources such as mills, trimming manufacturers, distributors and other collaborators in the supply chain who are audited and assessed. They need to provide vital management control for process safety, security and risk management. Audits focus on the policies and procedures to verify compliance with regulatory requirements and industry standards. The programmes must be properly designed and implemented as well as identify deficiencies and recommendations can be made as to where corrective actions may be required.

Audits are done by stages, the first being the gathering of information through visual observation, documented reviews and interviews with staff. This data is then compared to the regulatory requirements and an evaluation is made as to how they conform to the legal stipulations which forms part of the pre audit. The second phase of the audit would be an intense on-site inspection which includes the conducting of interviews and review of records to assess the effectiveness of the implementation of programmes. Lastly the post audit consists of the briefing of management on the findings and the prepartion of a final report and the relevant rating with corrective action recommendations.

Such audits should be conducted on an annual basis by a recognized audit company such as SMETA, WRAP or SA 8000. This should be followed up by physical visits to the plants. Audits are not limited to the point of manufacture but ought to also include the raw material sources, processing houses or any other out sourced functions at other vendors.

It is important that such reports are kept on record and up to date as in the event of a disaster such as a fire, building collapse or accident they will serve as critical points of reference.

Supplier introduction

Prior to commencing business with a new supplier it is required that the retailer briefs the supplier on all aspects of conducting business with them. This will apply to all processes that are in place to get them up and running and what is needed to be adhered to in order to maintain healthy relations thereafter.

The type of information that should be provided to the supplier is the background of the retail company and the philosophies as well as the type of operations in place so that they have a high level understanding of the company values that are subscribed to.

The supplier needs to have a crystal clear understanding of the end to end process which must be followed to become a certified supplier. This process will include the complete account registration, bank details and references, contractual agreements, settlement of payment terms and conditions and subscription to any software programmes that may be required to conduct business.

All conditions and guidelines in doing business should be outlined in a manual so that there is a detailed point of reference in the event of any dispute that may arise. Often the manual and other relevant information is available on the retailer's website for easy reference as is any training material together with ongoing updates and communications. The site may be access controlled even to the point that the information available is specific to the supplier. An example of such information is where the supplier is able to monitor the sales performance of their product in real time. It is essential that the channels of communication are structured and very clear as poor exchange of information has a negative impact and causes additional cost through wasted time, effort and resources which could result in late deliveries which will undoubtedly reflect in the end as lost sales.

Processes should be outlined for support and training usually in the form of instruction guides or is done practically in a lecture room environment. Representative topics would be for example, best practices for picking and packing, processing of orders and reporting availability of product. More technical training could be the procedures for the use of specific software packages, analysis and use of management reports or the use of a product critical management tool.

Performance management reports of the supplier should also be available in order that any shortcomings may be addressed promptly and enable the supplier to improve the efficiency of their operation. The type of key performance indicators that are measured, reported on and tolerances set are the analysis of customer returns, the measurement of actual variances to ordered quantities, the accuracy of picking and packing of product as well as the lead times of deliveries between receipt of orders and delivery to the retailer's receiving point.

A vital point to be measured is the rate of attrition during the production process which is the loss of product through rejects, under production through short delivery of raw materials or pilferage in the factory which results in loss of sales and needs to be analysed to keep these pre delivery instances to a minimum.

Customer returns must not only be quantified but the nature of the complaints have to be categorised and thresholds set to determine when a bulk return to supplier is warranted. The real danger lies where it is essential to retain the brand integrity when the nature of the defect can be considered dangerous or maybe life threatening and requires urgent withdrawal of the product from all points in the supply chain as well as the need to communicate a recall of the affected product through the media.

Where tolerances are set and the agreed criteria are not met, a consequence of some form or other may well be applied which usually has a financial implication through penalty discounts being enforced, rejection of delivery and the implementation of sale or return agreements.

Supplier manuals

The topics and information which is usually covered in the manual that may well form part of the memorandum of agreement are as follows

- The process that has to be followed to set up an account and the registration of the administrative details such as contact details, payment terms and logistical addresses. Retailer contact and help desk information is also published.
- Where the retailer may have unique software programmes for the conducting business such as the processing of orders, reporting of stock availability, the transfer of delivery instructions and product critical path management may require the supplier to invest in the packages and if need be upgrade the hardware to meet specifications to run such packages.
- All details of systems and reports generated should be described in sufficient detail to allow the supplier to be able to refer to in order to resolve any queries they may have.
- The manual must outline technical guidelines and testing requirements as well as packaging specifications and approved suppliers should be listed.
- Invoicing methods and the information that needs to be appear on such documents as well as the payment channels and methods have to be described in detail.

- Ticketing details, ticket examples, reference numbers and order process should appear together with a list of approved ticket printing houses as well as the consequences which are in place should goods be delivered without or with incorrect ticketing.
- Packaging specifications should be itemised with regard to outer cartons, pack quantities, sealing guidelines, weight tolerances and markings which have to appear on the cartons.
- The guidelines and processes that need to be followed to complete the delivery of product to the retailer's receiving point in terms of equipment handling, time slot booking, descriptive labelling and the like must be described in detail.
- The shipping documents utilised and the information that is required for off shore need to be noted as well as any specific administration processes that have to be followed.
- A detailed description is included of performance indicators and tolerances that are measured.
- The penalty levels which are applied where performance criteria are not met should be clearly stated in the manual as well as the methodology of the calculation to avoid disputes if and when the occasion arises.

Typical contractual contraventions are where the supplier's quality is found to be substandard and to be eligible for penalisation. Examples are quality failures in production, in cases where the safety of the product is compromised in the form of needle points or staples being found in the product, the use of poor attachments which carry the danger creating sharp edges on the garment that may pose a hazard to the consumer and the subcontracting of production to unauthorised vendors.

Clear guidelines and procedures as to the disposal of product need to be stated in the instances of the total withdrawal of product, production overruns, rejects and after what time period and which labelling or ticketing must be removed. Options that exist will be agreed on by the two parties for settlement of claims, for example, it may not be viable to incur reverse logistical costs to return distressed goods back to offshore suppliers and would be better to dispose of them locally. The recovery value would then be part of the settlement agreement with the supplier.

Protection of the retailer's intellectual property must be made very clear to all suppliers and this will pertain in the main to the safety of patents such as those relating to invention, utility or design. Trademarks are unique names, phrases, logos, symbols and can include colours which appear on the products themselves that are undoubtedly associated with the brand.

In the same way that the focus of the manual is on how to do things, the other side of the coin which is as important is the procedures to follow in order to exit from a supplier for whatever reason. It is not simply a case of no longer issuing orders and ceasing contact as there are certain processes which need to be clearly followed and signed off. These will include the deregistration of the account, the removal from all communication channels such as email distribution lists, elimination from access to any sensitive information on company websites and formal notification to all interested parties such as logistics, technology, marketing and financial departments.

Style briefing

Initially the supplier will be briefed conceptually what the product entails. The key information that is communicated is typically a sketch, photo, CAD print or sample with details. The detail will indicate design features, entail fabric and finish qualities, measurement guidelines, size range and ratios, colour ways, pricing and number of deliveries.

It is important that the supplier is provided with as much information as possible that is easily understood by even the most junior staff of the supplier especially in cases where English is not the first language. A principle of over communication and simplification should be followed to ensure complete clarity.

Meetings need to be handled professionally and follow a well prepared agenda and response to any queries have to be concise, well communicated and understanding needs to be tested. Detailed minutes and action plans with time scales attached should be clearly documented. Apart from the formal meetings, ongoing communications can be conducted via Skype and e-mail threads or conference calls.

Other information that can be included on a product specification document apart from the general information above is that pertaining to the inner packing, inserts and labelling. The product packaging minimum requirements and the methodology of the packing must be of a quality to withstand the rigours of transport, varying temperatures, inter warehouse transporting and mechanical handling.

A simple example of a style briefing sheet would look as follows

STYLE BRIEF		DATE	1 March
DEPARTMENT	Ladies T-Shirts	SUPPLIER	ABC
REFERENCE NUMBER	12345678	MNFR NUMBER	44455
DESCRIPTION	Ladies T-Shirt	SILHOUETTE	Top
DELIVERY DATE	20 September	NECKLINE	Round
UNITS	1,000	SLEEVE	Short
SIZES	Small 20% Medium 50% Large 30%	FIT	Regular
COLOURS	White 40% Beige 30% Red 30%	PRICE	129.00
FABRIC / YARN	100% Cotton Single Jersey Quality 12345	PHOTO / SKETCH	
STYLE COMMENTS	Piping must be contrast white.		

Specification pack

The product specification pack is the detailed briefing document used to clearly communicate the product details to the buying, design and technical teams as well as suppliers.

Components of the product specification pack

The type of information that should be included is

A sketch or digital picture, the season, the product name and reference number, fabric technical information, fit specifications, size details, quantities, sample sizes, delivery dates, packaging and placement of ticketing, outer packaging requirements, display materials such as hanger reference number, folding guidelines, details of required stitches and seams, trim card and placement details, garment sewing instructions, etc.,

This will enable the supplier to produce a first sample and provide a detailed quote of cost price.

The technologist will be responsible to provide the bill of materials, the test requirements for the fabric, trim and product, any finishes that are required, safety requirements, fit and block stipulations, wash care instructions as well as provide an assessment of the supplier capabilities to produce the product.

Supplier meetings

Once the product specification pack is formulated for a particular style, the retailer is in a position to initiate detailed meetings in order to prepare the supplier prior to the commencement of the production process.

It is extremely important that the meetings are well structured, prepared with an agenda, are clear and professional. Most importantly it is critical that the appropriate people are assigned tasks and completion dates are recorded for follow up.

Live information capture using a laptop and projector is very effective as meetings tend to be shorter, decisions and assignments are clear and results can be managed and tracked. The other advantage is that the publication of the minutes is immediate with the action tasks for those accountable being explicitly defined with completion dates.

Negotiating

Negotiation is the process whereby through dialogue between two or more parties an agreement is met and the outcome satisfies the needs of both within the boundaries that the situation will allow.

In the retail environment, negotiations typically revolve around topics such as price, garment content, costs, innovation and profitability. The discussions can take place under high pressure where the expectations of both parties are elevated and the rivalry is intense. Often the relationship may be under threat which may or may not add another dimension depending how significant the association is. The opposite of this can be, and the most suitable, where the two parties collaborate to reach the most desired outcome.

To achieve a situation where both parties benefit, requires maturity, a clear understanding of the end objectives with informed discussions by both parties and the development of a plan to achieve a mutual objective.

Notwithstanding the above the supplier and the retailer will still have their own agendas. The supplier will wish to sell as much as he can for the best price while the retailer will want the product for as cheap as possible for the best quality. If the retailer does not have an insightful understanding of the manufacturing process the chances are that they might end up paying too much or sacrificing content.

Negotiating can be a traumatic experience and not all may have the appetite for the heightened discussion. In the case of the supplier there could be a tendency to avoid the confrontation and at times simply give the product to the retailer for the price requested, while the retailer, on the other hand, will similarly pay the supplier's more expensive proposal without exploring all options to get the best deal.

The retailer must always be well prepared with all relevant facts regarding fabric, trim, ratings and costs, prevailing exchange rate trends, wage structures, margin policies including other external and internal factors at hand in order to be able to have an informed sincere discussion. The persuasion process must be done in a way that the argument is convincing and the acceptance by the other party is seen to be mutually beneficial, trustworthy and incorporates the other participant's needs.

The progression of negotiation follows the steps of preparation, conducting the discussion and reviewing the outcomes.

Thorough preparation is critical which requires that the issues and opportunities are identified, prioritised and have a value for both parties. Focus must be on both the hard subjects such as the monetary issues and volumes as well as the softer matters such as perceptions.

Boundaries must be set in the types of outcome broken up into which would ideally like to be achieved, or what is likely to be achieved and thirdly the bare minimum that would be accepted.

Analysis of the environment of both businesses must be well defined in terms of the markets, competitor activities and the supplier capability and technical expertise required. These factors coupled to the trading history and what percentage the supplier is of the retailer's business and what the retailer represents of the supplier's total production or put differently, who needs who the most.

Past performance and consistency as well as the growth potential and the degree of product uniqueness or cost advantages are important leverage factors that are to be taken into consideration.

Key bargaining points for the retailer are cost prices, discounts, volumes, exclusivity, return policies, promotional support, delivery scheduling and any other unique service while the supplier's focus is likely to be the volumes that can be achieved, the highest cost price that will be agreed and the long term sustainability of regular business.

There is not always a satisfactory resolution to negotiation discussions and contingency plans need to be in place as to what alternatives are available should a deadlock situation be reached. These may include the possibility of moving production to different suppliers, reduce volumes and increasing the levels of other substitution ranges, the consideration of sale or return agreements and although not desirable, possibly increasing the selling price above the norm.

Behaviour and strategies during the meeting are extremely important. Asking for more than is expected will give room for negotiation to what is acceptable without simply accepting the first offer. It is also essential to remain flexible and creative in an effort to avoid a deadlock situation. A vital point to bear in mind is that at all costs to avoid haggling as this practice runs the risk of destroying a relationship.

If confrontation does transpire, it should be tactically done and at all costs does not include any personal attack or involve the use of threats and ultimatums. The power of silence should be remembered as it can be effective and if needs be, try and concede to small bits at a time, park potentially unresolvable issues even if it means that the meeting has to be temporarily adjourned.

There are personal factors that can influence the final negotiation. Different partakers follow different processes, they have diverse experience levels as well as possess varying understandings and personality traits which may be unpredictable.

There is an added complexity in dealing with off shore suppliers where there are duties, logistical challenges, and culture and language differences.

Once the negotiations are concluded, a documented summary of the agreements, commitment of resources, capacity to deliver and action plans is absolutely critical to ensure complete understanding. The record will enable an amicable resolution should any misinterpretation which could possibly become a point of dispute at a later stage.

Costings

It goes without saying that cost forms an integral part of the negotiation process. It is therefore imperative that the retailer has a good understanding of the components and the proportions of a costing sheet thus permitting the ability to test the validity and understanding of any costing presented by a supplier.

The cost of a product is broken down into two distinct categories, namely direct product costs and the costs associated in getting the completed product to the retailer.

Factors that will influence the cost of a product will be the size ratio, which if weighted towards the larger sizes will utilise more fabric or affect the wastage of fabric because of a less efficient marking of the lay of fabric on the cutting table.

The level of detail of the styling may not only affect fabric consumption, it will probably also influence the manufacture time or minute rating.

The width of the fabric can also affect the usage of fabric and the general rule is that the narrower the width of fabric the more expensive the product is likely to be. Specialist fabrics tend to be on narrow width such as 110cm while the full width is 148cm. Woven fabrics can be as wide as 160cm.

Plain or printed fabrics will also affect fabric usage particularly where stripes need to be matched on different components such as sleeve and body and is likely to result in more wastage of fabric.

The components of the cost of the products can be divided into those that are considered to be fixed such as raw materials, overheads which include services such as design, technology and logistics and those that are variable which are in the main the constituents that are squeezed down to meet the demands of the retailer like wages, working hours and production methods.

Packaging costs will also vary for different types of product. The size of the cartons required to transport the product is determined by the dimensions of height and width that must protect and accommodate the garment comfortably. The in store presentation requirements will also affect the overall cost from the point of view that allowance may be needed for hangers as well as additional swing tickets.

Where goods are imported, duties need to be taken into consideration. Duties are normally determined against the free on board value or in other words the cost to place it on the deck of the ship. They can also be calculated as ex works which is the cost as at the completion of production.

Exchange rates are a critical factor. The option to purchase currency ahead of time at a fixed rate to finance the cost provides the peace of mind that the costs will be stable even if the day to day rates fluctuate. If currency is not bought ahead but goods are purchased at the prevailing rates the retailer may be forced to revise selling prices to ensure the achievement of the target margin.

Different categories of products attract different tariff duties at the receiving country depending on country of origin and manufacture as well as protection policies of local production.

The cost to transport the goods from the place of manufacture will vary for local goods or from the port by the clearing agent, depending on the location of the retailer in relation to the supplier or port, the size of the cartons or container and the mode of transport. Included in this section would be freight and warehousing charges.

198

The typical elements of a product costing and examples of approximate proportions will be

ELEMENT	DEPENDENCY	CATEGORY
TRANSPORT 5%	Different methods of transport used.	Transport / landing 20%
DUTY 30 - 40%	Taxes levied against the import of goods as specified by the local government.	
SUPPLIER MARGIN 10%	Supplier margin can vary between 5% and 15%.	
WASH AND TRIMS 5%	Costs allocated to special processes or trims.	
PACKAGING 7%	Total cost of all packaging, including presentation.	Production costs 80%
LABOUR 28%	The standard minute rates will differ from country to country, depending on operational complexity.	
FABRIC AND MATERIAL 50%	Will be influenced by the garment rating, which will dictate how much fabric is used to manufacture the garment.	

In addition to the product costs as outlined above there are other costs that need to be taken into account in order to get product to market. These can be categorised basically into two categories, firstly being additional costs to the supplier such as the base overhead costs being the total for rent, electricity, administration costs and the like that will always be there and which must be apportioned per product unit.

The second category can be described as being unrelated to the product directly that have to be paid. The main type of such costs are settlement discount agreements, marketing contributions, finance costs and royalties. These together with the product costs will deliver the final cost of the garment.

Points to note in the review of costs are in cases where the supplier throws in vague and unsubstantiated reasons to justify increases. It is essential that the retailer tests such requests to ensure they carry merit.

A typical instance is where the statement is made that wages have gone up and a new costing is proposed. A cross check is required to determine the proportion of what labour represents of the total costing. In the above example this would be the 28% for labour and apply the increase to this part and reconcile to the proposal.

Where increases are attributed to material increases an effort should be made to investigate the trend in the industry and do some comparisons even if they may be a bit crude. If your research shows that the increase is not in line with the trend, the supplier should be encouraged to find a better source and not to pass on the cost of their inefficiencies.

The use of exchange rate fluctuations to motivate cost price changes is more easily resolved as the average movement can be tracked over a period of time and applied. It is a possibility that in fact there might have been an improvement. Foreign currency could also have an influence depending at what price the supplier or retailer may have covered forward.

If the retailer's volumes are increasing significantly the opportunity exists to negotiate a discount in cost price to share the benefits of the improved scale of efficiencies. A point to note is that while this practice is not discouraged, the smaller retailer may not be able to finance the larger volumes of product or growth based incentives. Even with the benefit of a greater margin, the viability remains to be dependent on the organic growth of the chain, for example, the addition of new stores in order to accommodate the higher buying volumes.

A costing approach which is often employed by retailers is that of requesting appropriate suppliers to tender for a product. In order that this is done fairly and equitably the exact same specifications need to be provided to the potential suppliers. Cross costing comparison between suppliers is a popular option where there are large programmes up for grabs and is unlikely to be used for once off high fashion inputs.

For a retailer to commit to high volume programmes, it is a key requisite that the potential suppliers fulfil some basic requirements in that they must be financially stable, have a reliable track record in terms of delivery performance, provide consistent quality with up to date compliancy audits and will be able to cope with the required volumes which could include the agreement to hold a minimum stock holding. The supplier should also be flexible enough to be able to make styling changes to the product where necessary.

The key stipulations for use with cross costing or tenders which will be provided is a detailed style sheet, comprehensive specifications of fabric and trims, the garment measurements with the range of sizes, volumes, a target cost price, packaging requirements and packing methods, delivery dates or production flow.

ORDERING

After the negotiations are completed and the decision to award the production of a style to the supplier is taken, an order has to be drafted to reflect the commitment to the supplier.

The signed order for the supplier is created and placed by the retailer for the entire season in the case of a continuity product or possibly monthly for input styles. It is imperative that it must be done timeously to ensure the required completion date is realistically achievable and the production lead time required will be determined by careful critical path production management.

While the order is in essence a contractual document it will be subject to the overall terms and conditions that are entered into in a memorandum of agreement that is drawn up separately when a manufacturer is appointed as a certified supplier. Production can only commence once the final approved order is in the possession of the supplier.

The contract or the order is the document that details the terms by which the retailer takes ownership of the goods in exchange or payment of an agreed price.

The timing of orders is done according to the range plan guidelines and each supplier will be provided with an extract specific to them for the season. This production programme will indicate the style details, quantities, size ratios and colour specifications which will enable them to plan the production capacity and will be used as the point of reference during follow up production progress meetings. Each style will also have a corresponding style specification sheet which confirm the costs, pack quantities, labels and tickets, wash and care details, testing requirements and the fabric as well as component information.

Orders may be amended where required. These adjustments are normally for quantities, dates, prices and size ratios. The changes need to be recorded on the contract and refer to the date of the alteration as well as the nature of the change.

It is advisable that any style changes require the order to be cancelled and be replaced by a new order as in essence it is a different product.

The order can have two status phases where a pre-production contract enables the supplier to procure fabrics, components, labelling and packaging and make a pre-production or pre shipment sample which will be submitted to the retailer for approval. The sample will serve as the set standard of quality that will be referred to should any disputes evolve in production or in stores.

Production may only commence once a final approved order is received by the supplier.

Documented programmes of continuity lines for the full season may serve as an authorised arrangement from which the supplier will be able to order the raw materials and components but they will only be able to commence production of agreed quantities, for example, for six weekly time periods upon the receipt of an approved contract. This gives the retailer the flexibility to make adjustments based on current performance. Such amendments may take the form of changes to quantities, size ratios and colour quantities.

Dependent on whether the supplier is local or offshore the delivery requirements need to be clearly outlined with all relevant contact details, delivery stipulations, carton markings and delivery addresses.

In the case of a local supplier, delivery is normally to a designated warehouse at an approved time. Off shore suppliers may have to deliver to an offshore centralised consolidation centre where the goods will be amalgamated by shipping agents into containers prior to shipping. Payment will be made in the foreign currency and will be dictated by the international commercial (INCO) terms applied.

Common INCO terms for the payment of imported goods will be FOB (Sea Freight) which is where payment is prior to shipment by sea either by bank wire or a letter of credit. The purchaser's bank releases payment upon receipt of certain documentation such as the bill of lading, packing lists or commercial invoice and is due when the goods are loaded on the ship and ownership is then transferred to the retailer. If the INCO term is FCA it carries the same conditions as FOB except that the transportation is by air.

CFR (Sea and Air Freight) describes the situation where the supplier is responsible for the costs of transport to the destination port. While ownership only transfers when the goods reach the destination, the retailer is responsible for the goods while they are in transit and therefore they would have to take out insurance for this period. If the supplier does this then the INCO term applied is CIF (cost, insurance, freight).

Added to the costs are government duties which can be applied in the form of a percentage dependent on the various customs categories that the product falls into.

In terms of air freight it should be noted that the cost is often prohibitive as it is dictated by volume and weight and therefore is usually only applied to small and high value items or where an urgent stock need is required in order to meet a launch date.

When placing orders for imports it is critical to take into account the lead times that need to be added on to ensure the required delivery and launch dates are met. Lead time can be described loosely as the time that it takes for product to be delivered from the factory to the back door of the retailer's warehouse or distribution centre. This becomes increasingly complex when the factory is off shore as there are a whole host of additional activities that have to take place before the retailer eventually receives the goods.

 Pre shipment activities may involve the delivery to an off shore consolidation centre where different orders may be combined to make the full use of a container cost effective. Part deliveries in different containers can also make the consolidation and sequence of packing more complicated where there are different orders possibly also for different retailers.

In terms of the pre shipment critical path that needs to be adhered to prior to shipment is triggered by the supplier's confirmation that this will be met about three weeks before the ship date and approximately a week later the forwarder will advise the vessel and booking details at which time the supplier will send the pre shipment sample to the retailer with quality audit reports to request approval to ship.

A typical order for imported and local products will probably be as follows

ORDER									
RETAILER XYZ									

ORDER NO		DATE		
SUPPLIER		ORDER STATUS	Pre production	Production
SUPPLIER REFERENCE		COMPLETE/SHIP DATE		
PAYMENT TERMS		LAUNCH DATE		
DELIVERY METHOD		PACK QUANTITY		
DELIVER TO		TOTAL QUANTITY		
		COST VALUE		
		SELLING VALUE		

SKU NUMBER	STYLE NUMBER	STYLE DESCRIPTION	COLOUR	TOTAL COLOUR UNITS	SIZE	TOTAL SIZE UNITS	COST PRICE	SELLING PRICE
100023564	12345	Basic t-shirt	White	1000	S	200	45.00	99.99
100023565					M	400	45.00	99.99
100023566					L	300	50.00	110.00
100023567					XL	100	50.00	110.00
100023568	12345	Basic t-shirt	Black	2000	S	400	45.00	99.99
100023569					M	800	45.00	99.99
100023570					L	600	50.00	110.00
100023571					XL	200	50.00	110.00

BUYER SIGN		MANAGEMENT SIGN				
MERCHANDISER SIGN		SUPPLIER SIGN			DATE	

The information typically included on the order is as follows and will be stored on a data base system for any interested party that needs to access the detail.

Supplier reference number and name

Order number

Date that order was raised

Shipment date and launch dates

Shipping method

Method of payment

Point of delivery

Style number

Style description

Colour break down and quantity

Labelling instructions

Special terms or conditions of trade

SKU number

Size breakdown

Quantities

Number of units per inner pack

Number of inner packs per outer carton

Cost Price less any negotiated discounts

Selling Price

Signatures of authorization to buy are most commonly those of the buyer, merchandiser and a member of senior management. The omission of any of the signatures could result in the order being rendered invalid in the case of a disagreement. A supplier signature is often the rule but the acceptance of the order is in essence the recognition of all the terms and conditions of the order.

It is not uncommon for planning production schedules or provisional orders to be handed over to the supplier prior to the issuing of an official order, particularly in the case of replenishment product where the supplier needs to plan capacity requirements, order raw materials and components but this is by no means the go ahead to commence production. Without the completed signed order no knife may be put to the fabric.

The higher level order may be supplemented by a detailed specification pack and a critical path management document that serves as an appendage to the order and reflect the details and quality references of the fabric and components, sample submission requirements, technical tests, labelling instructions, packaging reference numbers and specifications.

The buying and merchandising team will use the basic information to interrogate orders at any time to check, monitor and if required will amend the orders which may be, for example, quantity or date related. Other areas of operation or parties will also need to have access to orders in order that their activities are completed timeously to safeguard that the final completion date is met.

Technology has to utilise the detail to ensure in the process of managing the critical path that all tests, quality control during the manufacturing process, garment fittings and rail samples are completed timeously.

The finance department need to know all the costing details and terms of payment as well as the proposed selling price to ensure that there is sufficient cash flow available to enable payment and be able to monitor the achievement of the gross profit margins.

The IT departments need to be aware of all orders for the provision of the SKU numbers as well as cater for the generation of the swing tickets or labels that are attached to the garments indicating the style number, colour, size and price detail which are either sent to the suppliers in bulk or the data files are transmitted to those suppliers that have the facilities to generate their own SKU tickets.

The distribution centre must have sight of the orders in the pipeline to assess the size of proposed deliveries going forward to ensure that they are in a position to plan sufficient resources in terms of staffing, equipment, space capacity and that sufficient transport is booked to deliver the goods speedily to stores.

CRITICAL PATH MANAGEMENT

In order to guarantee the on time launch of the product it is important to manage the path of product development. Without this the retailer ends up flying blind and often only finds out about delays from the supplier close to the expected delivery date when it is invariably too late to take corrective action.

All stakeholders involved in the process, which includes the buyers, suppliers, product technologists, fabric technologists and commercial management need to focus on the critical path management of the product.

There are on line order management systems available via the internet which enables the retailer to communicate globally with suppliers in order to track the progress of the product from the sampling stage through to delivery. This facilitates complete transparency while also highlighting the ramifications of poor decision making and poor capacity management.

The key stages or milestones which are in the main controlled by the buyers and technologists that need to be scrutinised are the style briefing and finalisation, colour approval, fit approval, bulk test of fabrics and components, approval of the pre-production sample, pre-production meetings with the supplier and final approval of the pre-shipment or rail sample prior to production at which point the product development can be considered complete and the launch date can be confirmed.

The monitoring of the process needs to documented and highlighted in some form in order that key players are able to measure the actual accomplishment of tasks compared to the required completion dates.

The purpose of such reports is not only to ensure that the critical milestones are met on time but also serve as a reference for meetings to identify possible delays and decide what actions need to be taken to improve or correct the situation.

In principle the lead times are measured in weeks and the relevant dates are attached starting from launch date which represents zero days and progressively working backwards taking the time for the completion of each stage into account and ending up where the no later than date for the starting style brief stage is determined.

The hierarchy of the reporting and performance measurement is done at style level and all the styles for a department can be rolled up to departmental level and then up to group level. These together with supplier extracts and other filters make for effective performance management of both the retail teams and the supplier.

PRODUCT DEVELOPMENT MANAGEMENT						Total	Pre-production sample & supplier meeting		Pre-shipment sample		Launch Date	
Supplier	Grp	Dept.	Style	Colour		Total	Complete	In-complete	Complete	In-complete	Complete	In-complete
abcd	1	123	44445	Black	Units	1000	750	250	750	250	750	250
					%	100	75%	25%	75%	25%	75%	25%
					Weeks	39	2		2		0	
					Date	10-Oct	06-May		17-Jun		01-Jul	
Supplier	Grp	Dept.	Style	Colour		Total	Complete	In-complete	Complete	In-complete	Complete	In-complete
abcd	1	123	55555	White	Units	1500	1500	0	1450	50	1500	0
					%	100	100%	0%	97%	3%	100%	0%
					Weeks	35	8		2		0	
					Date	10-Oct	06-May		17-Jun		01-Jul	
Supplier	Grp	Dept.	Style	Colour		Total	Complete	In-complete	Complete	In-complete	Complete	In-complete
bcde	2	124	55556	Yellow	Units	2000	1800	200	1700	300	1900	100
					%	100	90%	10%	85%	15%	95%	5%
					Weeks	35	8		2		0	
					Date	10-Nov	06-Jun		17-Jul		01-Aug	
Supplier	Grp	Dept.	Style	Colour		Total	Complete	In-complete	Complete	In-complete	Complete	In-complete
cdef	3	128	44445	Green	Units	1000	850	150	950	50	950	50
					%	100	85%	15%	95%	5%	95%	5%
					Weeks	39	8		2		0	
					Date	10-Dec	06-Jul		17-Aug		01-Sep	

PRODUCT DEVELOPMENT MANAGEMENT						Total	Style Brief		Style Finalised		Colour Approved		Fit Approved	
Supplier	Grp	Dept.	Style	Colour		Total	Complete	In-complete	Complete	In-complete	Complete	In-complete	Complete	In-complete
abcd	1	123	44445	Black	Units	1000	900	100	800	200	900	100	750	250
					%	100	90%	10%	80%	20%	90%	10%	75%	25%
					Weeks	39			28		24		11	
					Date	10-Oct			17-Dec		15-Jan		15-Apr	
Supplier	Grp	Dept.	Style	Colour		Total	Complete	In-complete	Complete	In-complete	Complete	In-complete	Complete	In-complete
abcd	1	123	55555	White	Units	1500	1300	200	1400	100	1450	50	1500	0
					%	100	87%	13%	93%	7%	97%	3%	100%	0%
					Weeks	39			28		24		11	
					Date	10-Oct			17-Dec		15-Jan		15-Apr	
Supplier	Grp	Dept.	Style	Colour		Total	Complete	In-complete	Complete	In-complete	Complete	In-complete	Complete	In-complete
bcde	2	124	55556	Yellow	Units	2000	1500	500	1400	600	1600	400	1800	200
					%	100	75%	25%	70%	30%	80%	20%	90%	10%
					Weeks	39			28		24		11	
					Date	10-Nov			17-Jun		15-Feb		15-May	
Supplier	Grp	Dept.	Style	Colour		Total	Complete	In-complete	Complete	In-complete	Complete	In-complete	Complete	In-complete
cdef	3	128	44445	Green	Units	1000	700	300	900	100	800	200	750	250
					%	100	70%	30%	90%	10%	80%	20%	70%	25%
					Weeks	39			28		24		11	
					Date	10-Dec			17-Feb		15-Mar		15-Jul	

QUALITY MANAGEMENT

It is important to ensure that proper quality control is applied so that that the product presents well on the shop floor, fits well, wears well, washes well, is functional and represents value for money to avoid the loss of sales through customer returns or the depletion of units during production which results in under deliveries and ultimately lost sales. The points of quality control are conducted throughout the supply chain process which includes those prior to production, during in line production, at dispatch stage and on the shop sales floor.

A quality controller needs to possess certain qualities that will equip them to ensure that a thorough and complete monitor is done. The key attribute required is that of the need to pay attention to detail along with assertiveness and transparency. Tasks have to be conducted professionally and ethically. The incumbent must be prepared to be open minded and consider alternative points of view. The nature of the job requires tact and diplomacy and in certain situations the quality controller is required to be culturally sensitive. Decisiveness together with collaboration is paramount to ensure that quality standards are maximised.

Quality control starts with ensuring that the fabric being utilised meets the required specifications to be transformed into a perfect garment and therefore needs to be managed and inspected for faults which are marked. The length and width of fabric have to be checked to ensure that they meet the specified measurements and thereby do not affect the cutting table lay.

The supplier will need to have the fabric and trims tested by a recognised laboratory to record that they meet the weight, width and yarn specifications. Tests also need to focus on the performance of fabrics such as rub tests or how the fabric reacts in a washing machine in terms of colour fastness and shrinkage.

One of the critical objectives of the pre-production meeting which is conducted for every style is to set the standards to which the quality will be measured during production.

The pre-production sample serves as the basis of discussion and all key stakeholders will be present from both the retailer and the supplier. Technology representatives and the buying team must attend together with supplier teams to determine the criteria for sewing, finishing, fabric, trim, quality assurance, cutting, production and packaging management. At these meetings the technical requirements are stipulated and agreed for the make-up, sewing and thread combinations, the special methods that are needed to handle trims in bulk production, the wash and product finishing standards as well as the packaging and shipment methods. Any special processes out of the ordinary must be well documented and the minutes of the meeting must be recorded and signed off by all participants to ensure there are clear reference standards in the event of any difference that may transpire at a later stage.

If required it may be decided to produce wearer trials to assess the performance of the product in relation to the technological test standards especially where physical or chemical laboratory tests are not appropriate or it is not able to be spot checked in bulk production. All in all the purpose of the pre-production meeting is to identify risk areas which may result in product failure or possible injury to the customer and establish preventative measures.

In production the quality audits must include the assessment of care labels, packaging, price tags, colour and the quality of garment finishing and conformance to measurement specifications. The main visual checks will include the button attachments, non-inclusions of seams, fabric flaws, elastic failures, colour mismatches, poor make up and appearance. Safety issues such as needle points or staples in the product are also watched out for.

It is important that the audit report is completed speedily in order that preventative measures can be documented and action plans are implemented. The number of garments that must be measured and assessed is determined by agreeing the sample survey percentage that will represent the total quantity and what tolerances are allowed before rejection takes place.

It is assumed that 5000 pieces are purchased with the breakdown and sample survey quantities as follows

	WHITE	BLACK
SIZE M	1 500	1 200
SIZE L	1 500	800

Of the 5 000 units, it is agreed to check 30% visually and measure 10%

VISUALLY INSPECTED	WHITE	BLACK
SIZE M	450	360
SIZE L	450	240

MEASURED	WHITE	BLACK
SIZE M	150	120
SIZE L	150	80

Graphically the inspection sample can be depicted as follows

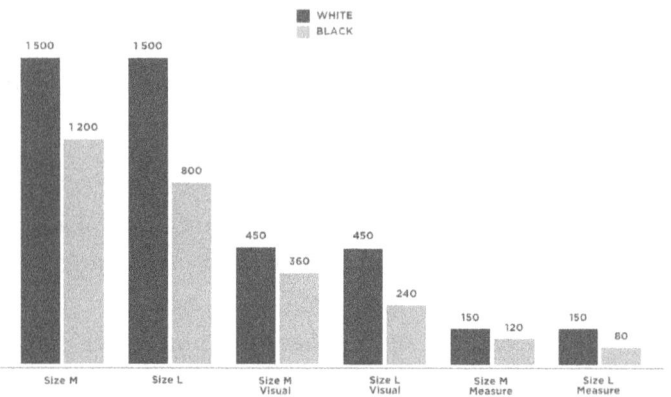

WHITE
BLACK

A typical measurement sheet will look like the example below

QUALITY MEASUREMENT AUDIT REPORT												
DEPARTMENT	XYZ	STYLE	STYLE DESCRIPTION									
COLOUR	WHITE	SIZE	SMALL				MEDIUM				LARGE	
OP NO	DESCRIPTION		SPEC (cm)	1	2	3	SPEC (cm)	1	2	3	SPEC (cm)	1	2	3
1	Across front		35				37.5				40			
2	1/2 chest		48				53				56			
3	1/2 hem		46				51				53			
4	Shoulder		13.5				14				16			
5	Overarm sleeve		18				21				23			
6	Underarm sleeve		7.5				9				11			
7	Across back		38				40				43			
8	Neck drop front		8.2				9.6				11			
9	Neck width		18.2				19				21			
10	Neck drop back		1.5				2				2.5			
INSPECTED BY			TOTAL MEASURED					COMMENTS				
			RESULTS									
SUPPLIER			Out of tolerance									
			In tolerance									

In addition to the production line audits it is also necessary to conduct quality inspection in stores which apart from identifying and resolving quality issues there is the added advantage of interacting with sales teams and share knowledge and learnings from those at the coal face who interact with the customer.

Apart from the skill levels and components which may affect the quality of a garment there are other factors which need to be taken into account. For Chinese suppliers it is important to consider production which takes place close to the Chinese New Year holidays. Not only is it the completion of orders prior to the commencement of holidays which could put pressure on the rate of production the other real risk is the start-up time taken by factories after the holidays. This is often a slow process due to the fact that many of the workers who travel inland to their villages are tardy in returning back to work or take extended leave which results in broken production and the use of lower skill levels to complete more complex operations. This phenomenon is part and parcel of doing business with Chinese suppliers and contingencies need to be put in place as invariably suppliers who do not have the capacity to complete orders on time which were optimistically accepted as well as the fact that raw material suppliers experience the same phenomenon also puts excessive strain on the production lines to meet deadlines timeously. In summary careful planning with built in safety stocks to ensure continuity of supply to the stores is paramount.

Environmental circumstances such as storms which prevent ships docking or deviate from their routes, power failures, strikes, goods being held up at customs or other unforeseen events can delay the arrival of raw materials and finished product and may impact eventually on the timing, quality and quantity being delivered.

SUPPLIER PERFORMANCE MANAGEMENT

The objective of achieving zero defects and delivering optimum quality is done through the building and sustaining of relationships by continually assessing, anticipating and fulfilling stated and implied needs.

The risks that can be encountered are aggravated in certain situations such as with the movement of strategic product to new plants, or existing suppliers being utilised for different types of products which they may not adapt well to. The allocation of high volumes with a minimal quality assurance infrastructure in place as well the ability to meet critical launch dates require that performance measurement is critical for early identification of any potential failure.

A tough line has to be taken on dealing with substandard delivery and quality. Data collected from various sources needs to be accurate and reliable especially where a penalty system is applied for non-performance.

Customer returns have to be analysed and criteria put in place which may result in a penalty being applied for the number of returns in the form of a sliding scale. The analysis of the most common faults also highlights the areas of quality which need to be addressed.

The late or under completion of orders or non-conformance to size and colour ratios translate directly to lost sales and can be assessed and penalized either through a direct fine or a trade discount and possibly a sale or return arrangement. A word of caution with regard to a sale or return arrangement is although the goods that are not sold after a period of time can be returned, the sales of these goods may impact the performance of other similar products that are on offer at the same time which is not always taken into account.

Late deliveries measurement ensures that completion is on time according to the critical path. A typical example of a penalty is one which is on a sliding percentage scale of discount for every week that the delivery date is missed up to a pre-determined stage after which the order faces cancellation.

Lead times can be measured based on the time taken for the supplier to deliver to the retailer's back door. A realistic number of days can be set as a tolerance for the delivery of product based on mode of transport and distance from the retailer thereafter penalties may be activated. It does happen that the supplier may report the full availability of product but in reality part of the order may still be in production and the delivery may take place in the form of a number of split drops which would be unacceptable and is almost equivalent to fraud.

Order fill percentage represents what was actually delivered in comparison to what was ordered. Any deviation to this translates into lost sales from the lowest size level as the retailer is not receiving what was ordered.

Ticketing must be accurate as an incorrect ticket which is scanned in will be captured erroneously on the stock data base and sales at the till point will be incorrect thus distorting the product's data integrity which will only be rectified once a physical product count is completed.

Sample checks upon receipt of product will help identify such errors and enforce the implementation of a penalty system. Often the attachment of incorrect SKU tickets could be as a result of poor communication and disciplines between the retailer and supplier, poor control at suppliers or non-destruction of old SKU tickets at times of a price changeover.

The advantage of a controlled performance management system is the quick identification of poor performing suppliers. The more efficient suppliers welcome the performance measurements as it assists supplier management to more effectively manage their business, assign accountability and also be able to assess their contribution to sales performance and strive to benefit from the advantage of incentive schemes applied by the retailer where they exist.

It is not surprising that the garment manufacturers are in turn also applying penalty systems and clauses in the contracts with their raw material suppliers such as the fabric mills and trimmings suppliers.

It is preferable that a reporting system is entrenched and is published on a monthly basis to the supplier and the internal buying groups. Such reports form a good basis of discussion in meetings with the supplier and alerts the buying team to potential problems that may be evolving. It should therefore be no surprise to the supplier if the need to apply penalties is necessary as sometimes the monetary value of the penalties could pose a major financial risk to a supplier.

Supplier meetings where qualitative feedback and their performance measures are discussed encourages commitment between the two parties and promotes collaboration. At such meetings the sales performance of the products specific to the supplier is analysed and understood. This may lead to the formulation of action plans where required and may include cooperation and coordination of marketing activities which could comprise of cooperative advertising and media campaigns. Part of the discussion would include the sharing of information regarding consumer, product, market trends and new innovations.

PRODUCT ALLOCATION

Once production is complete the supplier will advise via a report what volumes by size and colour are complete and packaged ready for dispatch to the addresses as stipulated by the retailer.

In a perfect world the intake will match the volumes as indicated on the intake line in the original plan as highlighted earlier.

The intake plan in monetary value was previously planned as follows

	TOTAL SEASON	MONTH 1				MONTH 2				MONTH 3				
		WK 1	WK 2	WK 3	WK 4	WK 5	WK 6	WK 7	WK 8	WK 9	WK 10	WK 11	WK 12	WK 13
OPEN STOCK	77 000	77 000	79 000	82 000	81 000	81 000	88 000	96 000	98 000	96 000	99 000	98 000	91 000	83 000
SALES	370 000	10 000	12 000	14 000	14 000	12 000	13 000	14 000	15 000	13 000	14 000	19 000	21 000	16 000
MARKDOWN	700				700									
INTAKE	376 700	12 000	15 000	13 000	14 700	19 000	21 000	16 000	15 000	14 000	13 000	12 000	13 000	15 000
FWD COVER		6	6	6	6	6	6	6	6	6	6	6	6	6
CLOSING STOCK	83 000	79 000	82 000	81 000	81 000	88 000	96 000	98 000	98 000	99 000	98 000	91 000	83 000	82 000

	TOTAL SEASON	MONTH 4				MONTH 5				MONTH 6				
		WK 14	WK 15	WK 16	WK 17	WK 18	WK 19	WK 20	WK 21	WK 22	WK 23	WK 24	WK 25	WK 26
OPEN STOCK	77 000	82 000	83 000	84 000	85 000	86 000	87 000	87 000	85 000	83 000	83 000	85 000	85 000	83 000
SALES	370 000	15 000	14 000	13 000	12 000	13 000	15 000	16 000	15 000	14 000	13 000	14 000	15 000	14 000
MARKDOWN	700													
INTAKE	376 700	16 000	15 000	14 000	13 000	14 000	15 000	14 000	13 000	14 000	15 000	14 000	13 000	14 000
FWD COVER		6	6	6	6	6	6	6	6	6	6	6	6	6
CLOSING STOCK	83 000	83 000	84 000	85 000	86 000	87 000	87 000	85 000	83 000	83 000	85 000	85 000	83 000	83 000

Sales will never be exactly as expected as the customers do not have prior knowledge of the plans and will always buy differently. Coupled to this the amount of over or under production due to a reject factor could result in availabilities being higher or lower than what the supplier was meant to make and therefore the actual closing stock at the end of each period will definitely vary to the expectation. Markdown values are also continually different to that planned.

Stocks and sales are the anchor targets that are consistently aimed for with the intake being the balancing variable to bring the plan back in line. In the hypothetical exercise below done for Month 1 of the plan it is illustrated as to how the intake is manipulated over the four weeks of the month in order to meet the original stock targets.

Intake adjustment to reconcile to target stocks

	TOTAL SEASON	MONTH 1			
		WK 1	WK 2	WK 3	WK 4
OPEN STOCK	77 000	77 000	79 000	82 000	81 000
ACTUAL OPEN STOCK	80 000	80 000	80 300	78 800	78 800
SALES	50 000	10 000	12 000	14 000	14 000
ACTUAL SALES	45 600	7 000	10 000	14 500	14 100
MARKDOWN	700				700
ACTUAL MARKDOWN	800			200	600
INTAKE	54 700	12 000	15 000	13 000	14 700
ACTUAL INTAKE	47 400	7 300	8 500	14 700	16 900
FWD COVER		6	6	6	6
ACTUAL FWD COVER		5	5	5	5
CLOSING STOCK	83 000	79 000	82 000	81 000	81 000
ACTUAL CLOSING STOCK	81 000	80 300	78 800	78 800	81 000

To summarise for the month, the total actual monetary value of sales missed target by 4400 and due to the fact that the actual stock opened higher than expectation by 3000 with 100 more markdown then target resulted in the intake for the month having to be reduced from a plan of 54700 to 47400.

It must be noted that the monetary intake requirement needs to be converted to units at the style/colour level to enable the stock availability to be allocated and distributed.

The allocation of product from the availability reports provided by suppliers or stocks stored in the warehouse takes on two methodologies. The input type products, usually for seasonal launches or fashion styles are described as "push" products while the continuity product which is replenished in empathy to sales performance are known as "pull" products where allocations are triggered by minimum stock level points and stopped by the maximum stock level thresholds.

The key differentiators of these types of products are that "push" styles cater for peak sales before being replaced. These styles attract a higher markdown volume as they are removed off display once the range becomes broken as they need to make way for the new themes that the replacement input styles bring.

"Pull" styles determine the requirements based on replacement of actual sales to a pre-determined build to level of stock. The calculation of the quantity of stock required will be the be determined by the amount of intake needed to meet the stock target that is either dynamically determined by the set weeks sales forward cover or is maintained at a static level over time.

"Pull" styles should typically be continuity items that have a predictable rate of sale and have a balanced availability of sufficient volumes of stock from the lowest level to meet the fluctuating demand. The supplier's production planning therefore has to be consistently reliable and flexible to sustain this condition.

The "pull" principle can be illustrated as follows

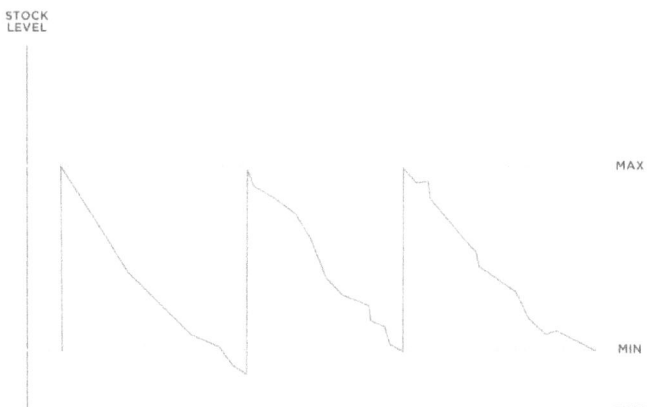

The automatic replenishment or distribution of products is often performed through the use of sophisticated technical allocation systems and are most suitable for the basic continuity product that have consistent predictable sales patterns and for store displays which are laid out according to a centralised space planning system.

The application needs to be merged with the historical sales data and the planned overall sales going forward. In order to achieve a constant replenishment over time a technique of smoothing is utilised where a weighting factor is applied to sales which deviate from the norm due to an unusual event and in such cases the system will use the adjusted realistic level of sale in the algorithm to derive the most appropriate forward allocations.

In the case where there is a launch of new lines, the new line can be linked to the pattern of a similar current style. The performance of the new styles must therefore be very carefully monitored early on and adjusted if need be to ensure the best size provision as possible.

The manual overriding of calculated allocations at store level should only take place in exceptional circumstances for specific reasons such as unforeseen special events, competitor activity or natural disasters. Often the temptation exists to manually override allocations based on an inherent gut feel and this should be avoided at all costs.

The delivery instruction which is sent to the supplier specifies the quantities that must be picked and packed per item per store by colour and size.

The primary size refers to the commonly designated size of all products such as waist measurements, neck and chest sizes while the secondary size refers to products which have other options of the main primary size such as different leg lengths for trousers or varying cup size options in case of bras.

If automated replenishment systems do not exist or are not very sophisticated it may occur that the actual sales by size do not mirror those as planned. In such cases it is necessary to review the size patterns using a manual technique and alter contract ratios going forward. A special balancing contract must be raised for production of those specific sizes that are short in order to realign the size sales pattern to that of the amended regular contracts going forward. A very clear indication where the size ratio is out of line is where at the end of range launches the left over stocks or reduced stocks are dominated by one or two sizes. If one applies one's mind to the consequence of this, it is a fact that potential sales have gone drastically astray of better selling sizes and profit is consequently not maximised.

In summary, the sad part about poor performers or the lack of stock control, is that especially in the case of high volume continuity styles, the resultant negative impact can be likened to a lingering illness that lives with the buying team until the situation of overstocks of unwanted product is eventually rectified or doomed to the reduced counter. It is therefore critical that where there is a hint of such an evolving scenario that very swift action is taken.

Where there has been above average performance of categories, a situation may arise where the amount stock available is unable to satisfy the requirements of the entire store catalogue. In such instances the predicament that exists is one of how to keep everybody happy. The choice usually boils down to reducing the quantities proportionately across the entire catalogue dependent on the priority of need whereby at least each store sees a piece of the pie before sell outs are experienced. The other option is to take the view to shrink the number of stores that are serviced and best satisfy the stores that are more likely to deliver the greatest volume of sales. In many cases it is not uncommon for twenty percent of the catalogue to deliver sixty to seventy percent of the sales. The selection of the second option will retain the credibility of the customers in the bigger units but will disappoint the many customers across the balance of the stores. A tactic to alleviate severe situations is by choosing a geographical cross section of stores and if an on-line facility exists, to ensure that stock is available at all times that can be ordered via the internet.

The use of digital imaging has helped develop realistic three dimensional representations which enable the product to be placed efficiently on the various types of equipment in the store. Such systems operate at detail size level so in theory a store will never be out of a size as the principle applied is that as the store sells one it gets one. The key to the success of such a system is that the data integrity has to be as accurate as possible. If this is not the case, for example, where the data base is distorted through incorrect barcode ticketing or pilferage will result in allocations being calculated inaccurately. The only means to rectify the data base is to do a disciplined full manual stock count from time to time and update the data base accordingly.

Delivery Instruction note example

ORDER NO	12345		DEPARTMENT	Men's Trousers
SUPPLIER	ABC Manufacturer		STYLE NO	5554
DATE	14 March, 2015		DESCRIPTION	Casual cotton trouser

		COLOUR	GREY					
	STORES	PRIMARY SIZE	32	34	36	38	40	42
		SECONDARY SIZE	32	34	36	38	40	42
NO	STORE	TOTAL	120	170	160	140	110	100
141	City Centre	250	38	53	50	44	34	66
145	Main Street	200	30	43	40	35	28	53
148	Back Street	250	38	53	50	44	34	66
151	Country Lane	100	15	21	20	18	14	26

PRODUCT STORAGE AND DISTRIBUTION

Logistical planning and supply chain

Supply chain logistics is described as the product movement comprising of the transport and shipment of goods from the point of origination and clearance through customs where applicable to the distribution centre or warehouse and on to stores where the goods are placed on offer for purchase to the customer. Many stores traditionally have stockroom facilities or at least a backroom to accommodate overflow stocks.

The reality is that the same rates of rental are charged as that for saleable metreage and therefore it is preferable that off-site storage facilities be maintained. The downside of holding stocks in high rental cost stock rooms is that invariably the remnant stocks of promotions or themes are removed from the sales floor and left in the stock room to gather dust waiting for the seasonal write down.

Out of season stocks such as thermal underwear are returned to the stockroom to await the reappearance of the next season to be returned to the sales floor. In such situations, particularly where there are undisciplined controls in the store, stocks get lost in the black hole of the stock room and bad or dead stock will accumulate and affect the data integrity of the stock records. It is therefore essential that redundant stocks are written off and cleared out almost immediately.

The trend is to keep store holding areas as small as possible and enable the regular drawing off from larger economical offsite storage facilities which can be done more effectively through a centralised point whether it be at the warehouse or in the commercial office. The success as to how well this is done is dependent on the responsiveness of the warehouse and reduces the accumulation of isolated pockets of stocks while minimising the corruption of stock data integrity as well as the reduction of double handling of merchandise.

Examples of stock held in the holding room is the accommodation of an overflow of stock where space planning is applied using planograms. End of ranges stock that have to be returned to the centralised storage facility or supplier may need to be held temporarily in the back room awaiting collection. Stock is also temporarily held for consolidation in back room areas until all components of a promotional launch is received and moved to the sales floor on the launch date for maximum impact.

The selection of the various options of supply chain will depend on a number of criteria such as the source of supply, characteristics of the product, the costs of the storage and distribution, selling locations, shelf life and customer demand.

The main channels of supply are a flow through model without storage or warehoused product. Outside of these channels the other formats are direct delivery to stores or displays being fully merchandised by the vendor.

The type of distribution model that is selected will depend on factors such as the size and growth phase of the retailer. For example, smaller or new retailers will probably prefer to operate a cross dock model which does not require investment in large warehouse facilities or the need to carry excessive inventory enabling their efforts to be focused possibly on opening more stores.

For a larger mature retail chain on the other hand, it may be essential to operate through a network of sophisticated warehousing amenities. These enjoy elaborate systems whereby they have better control of the management of the inventory and are able to efficiently allocate, pick and pack and schedule deliveries to stores country wide or even internationally.

Retailers also have the choice to manage their own facilities or outsource them. The main factor that is considered in selecting the most suitable option is the cost saving element. Initially it may have been cheaper to outsource without having to invest in the high setup cost of such an infra-structure, however, as the retailer grows, coupled to the fact that the third party is a profit based operation that delivers expertise in the warehousing field, the time will come when it is more beneficial to move the operation in house.

A workable compromise solution that is often employed is for the retailer to control their own warehouse facilities with the accompanying IT infrastructure and avoid the major upheaval should they change third parties but to still outsource the transport network part to specialised haulage service providers.

Cross dock or flow through model is the arrangement where the goods are pre picked and packed at the supplier and are delivered to the distribution centre with store labels already gummed on the boxes or hanging sets. The alternative model of cross dock is where the order across the stores is delivered in bulk by the supplier to the cross dock facility and the goods are picked by distribution centre staff and deposited directly in the respective store dispatch bays. Eventually the product from all suppliers for the day is consolidated in each store's designated bay awaiting transport.

Stores that are geographically far from the receiving distribution centre have the goods transhipped in bulk to their own respective closest geographical distribution centre where the picking operation will take place. The number of regional distribution centres will be largely dependent on the density of the store network and the operating costs of such facilities.

The added benefit of the goods being picked and packed at the supplier is that the cartons are able to contain a combination of size and colour requirements by store and will therefore eliminate the need to unpack and repack from warehouse stock thus eliminating double handling and is subsequently more cost efficient. It is also possible where the supplier is picking multiple styles for the same store that these can be nested in the same container which reduces the need for additional packaging as well as reduces handling making for a considerable time saving.

In the event that there are over or short deliveries these cause delays as the changed quantity requires that the computer is updated and the store quantities are scaled or recalculated based on varying algorithms that satisfy those stores with the greatest need first rather than simply apportioning equally across all the stores before the picking process can take place.

In the case where the receipt of product from suppliers is pre labelled for stores the testing of the accuracy is done by randomly inspecting a sample of cartons per supplier delivery and should the errors of packing fall outside of a certain tolerance it may result in the entire delivery being rejected. Where inaccuracies are within the tolerance but there is still a measure of incorrectness the error factor will still be extrapolated for the entire delivery and the invoicing is amended accordingly. Dependent on the size of the error it could attract a penalty. While many find this concept difficult to accept, it should be remembered that the time and cost to do a full unpack and reconciliation in all likelihood would render the operation to be considered impracticable. Tests have been statistically done which reveal that the deviation from the sample survey results is also not that large.

The advantage of a flow through supply chain type is that the allocation can be made as late as possible allowing the shortening of the lead time and thereby meeting the customer demand more efficiently. The other benefit is also that the storage space requirement is minimal and dependent on the payment obligation it may be beneficial to the retailer in terms of cash flow in that ownership is only transferred upon receipt at the distribution centre.

There is an argument that utilising cross dock without warehousing is possibly a disadvantage in terms of the speed of delivery to stores as having stock drawn from the warehouse is quicker and smoother than waiting for the supplier delivery. The challenge is therefore to streamline the supplier delivery efficiencies to avoid the cost impact of holding warehoused stock and the handling costs that accompany this option.

Other difficult situations arise where there is a poor performing unreliable supplier for which a contingency is required when they fail to deliver and similarly at key periods such as holidays where the factories shut down for a period and in spite of confirming that there will be a skeleton staff to cope with the execution of orders over this period the level of service is invariably diminished.

Example of a cross dock flow through model

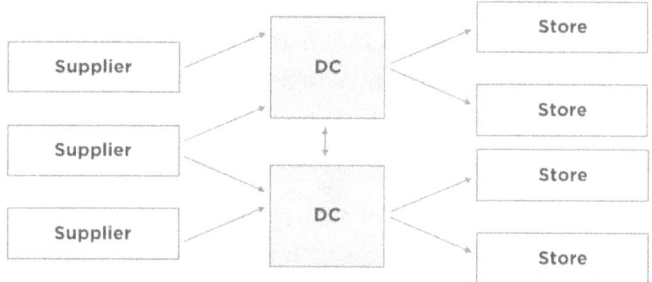

Warehoused product is where the goods are received in bulk and are held in storage awaiting a call off and distribution to stores or to other storage sheds using the cross dock facilities.

The warehouse can be seen to operate in a similar way as the supplier and performance management of indicators such as pick and pack accuracy, lead time measurement and the like can be implemented in the same way.

Warehoused stock tends to be predominantly for imported product but can also include local suppliers particularly where minimum order quantities or negotiated special volume deals apply. In the main the products are continuity items with long supply lead times which are replenished on a regular basis as "pull" allocations.

The challenge with warehouse stock is to manage the stock levels as the investment in high volumes does not only have adverse financial consequences but also a real physical problem can arise in the form of space constraints and the possible requirement of additional operational resources. There are also instances of seasonal goods such as knitwear being produced in the off season to maintain a consistent production throughout the year and therefore creates an accumulation of stocks in the warehouse either at the supplier or the retailer at a cost which needs to be accounted for.

A point to note is that the storage shelving location is restricted to a fixed size which is usually the size of a pallet and may be at multi levels. As goods are withdrawn to the pick and pack locations it does happen that within one storage location a lesser quantity of goods remain behind which results in the space utilisation not being optimal as two different SKU's are not able to share the same location. Technically the warehouse becomes restricted in the capacity availability while physically this may not be the case. Thought needs to be applied to the minimum percentage or quantity that is able to be efficiently maintained and what tactics must be utilised regarding the consolidation of and removal of such stocks to free up the storage slots. This may take the form of allocating the odds to stores or transferring it to a different storage area with smaller slots and take on a high priority for distribution thereafter.

Other space inhibiting practices are where there are poor rates of sales, or volume deals are negotiated or through minimum order quantities that are imposed which cause the warehouses to fill up eventually and consequently result in the total utilisation of palette slots. The alternative then remains to either source outside storage, put the brakes on in terms of accepting intake or to simply stop buying to relieve the space and financial strain. The consequences of this is that availabilities suffer with the disruption of the composition of product and theme launches as well as the service levels of suppliers decline when they put production on hold while they wait for the retailer's stock levels to diminish and inevitably will sell on to other competitors in order to keep their production capacity full and operational.

The siting and the number of warehouses will be reliant on the geographic network of stores, the proximity to suppliers and ports and will be dependent on the achievement of the most economical costs which need to be continually reviewed to ensure the delicate balance of viability is maintained. This balance is particularly important in the case of retail chains which continually open and close stores.

The introduction of higher levels of automation and the possibility of outsourcing operations to contractors or independent logistical organisations for storage and the management of the fleet of transport to tranship between storage points and schedule deliveries to stores also has an impact on the sustainability.

After the unloading of a container or truck at the back door, the cartons are consolidated and received, and then palletized for packing away in the storage facilities with unique identification location barcodes for ease of retrieval upon withdrawal in bulk.

After drawing product in bulk from the shelves the goods are moved to a pick and pack location to satisfy each stores order and are deposited in the unique store bays to await dispatch.

An alternative option is to pick and pack goods directly from storage shelves by store and when the order of the various products for each specific store is complete it is delivered to the store's relevant bay.

The appropriateness of which picking method to apply will depend largely on the size of the withdrawals. The larger volumes are usually removed to a picking area in bulk where the pick and pack operations take place. The smaller the quantities that are required by store, the picking by individual store across the product range into picking bins or shipping units for each store would probably be more suitable. It is possible that some retailer's employ both methods from different areas of the warehouse dependent on the product characteristics and volumes.

The task of picking is activated by the generation of a computer picking sheet which informs the picker as to which location must be accessed and indicates the quantity that must be withdrawn. Together with this the computer will create the store labels which is applied to the shipping container.

There are generally two methods of generating picking lists and labels. The more manual method is where the picking lists are generated up front prior to the picking operation but the downside is that it is susceptible to inaccuracies and at the end of the operation the computer needs to be updated manually and report any exceptions. The implication is that this step must be fulfilled before any goods can be shipped which could cause delays.

The other option is real time picking which is the technique of using hand held terminals that employ radio frequency to give the pickers their instructions on a computer terminal or pad. With the handheld terminal or voice instructions via hands free headsets the picker will scan the barcodes of the product and locations to confirm that the correct product has been identified and the picking can commence which will then update the stock data base in real time. For this reason the accuracy is almost guaranteed and the movement of stock is free flowing.

As all retailers are concerned about shrinkage this method is a big plus and also lessens the   possibility of disputes between the warehouse and stores with respect to over or short deliveries. The facility to automatically generate store delivery notes is provided enabling the deliveries to be tracked. Real time control does however come at a much added cost and therefore the viability must be assessed in terms of the benefits it brings with it.

There are sophisticated automated picking systems which lessen the manual handling of product but these require a higher level of investment. The most common system employed is a conveyer belt system whereby the pickers are relatively stationery and are responsible for a section of products in an area where the items are packed onto the conveyer belt from which picking takes place and can be done for either the store or product picking options.

Challenges that the picking operation faces is that different approaches are required to segment activities in cases where fast selling items need to be picked more frequently and others such as for some stores that require less service than others. Consequently there is a prerequisite to carefully schedule actions in order to streamline deliveries.

In a similar way the peaks and valleys of volumes through the week apply undue strain on the operation at certain times while at other spells the warehouse may stand idle. In the case of clothing where there are not many expiry dates involved the approach should possibly be to pick the high volume product outside the peak delivery periods and reserve the ability to prioritise the promotion items during the peak delivery period thereby smoothing the operation and maintain a constant labour utilisation.

The ideal size of the warehouse is difficult to assess but the general rule is obviously the smaller the warehouse the better as the overheads are kept to a minimum and experience often shows whatever the size of the shed is it will inevitably be filled. The size should be tailored to the space required during normal trading and not to accommodate peak periods such as Christmas or the accumulation of stock build up prior to Chinese New Year when at such times additional temporary space can possibly be procured or alternatively implement night shifts to keep stocks moving.

The flow of product within a warehouse environment is illustrated below

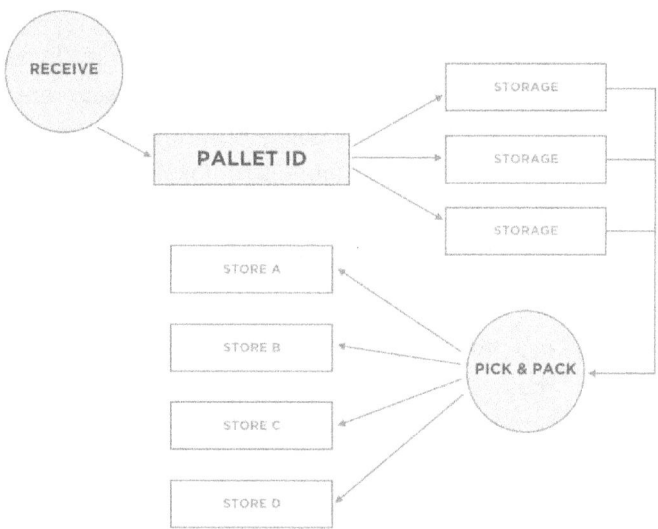

Direct delivery of product to the store location by the supplier is used where the retailer does not have the infrastructure to accommodate certain types of product such as high priced goods like cosmetics and expensive accessories.

This mode of delivery is also required where the vendor completes the end to end merchandising management of the displays whereby slow selling stock is withdrawn and replaced by the supplier. A typical example would be a product such as greeting cards, accessories and magazines.

In summary, a well-managed supply chain enables the retailer to acquire goods from the manufacturer more profitably, facilitate well controlled stock levels, and provide more timeous response to the consumer demand as well as the building of sustainable working relationships between the retailer and the supplier.

VALUE ADDED PROCESSING

The need for additional work on product is frequent and the facilities to do this has to be provided for to make goods store ready. The nature of value added work can take on a variety of forms but typical examples are as follows.

Goods that are received from off shore suppliers may be bulk packed or not be received in their final form in order to achieve optimum space utilisation during transit. Prime examples of this is in the case of cushions or duvets which are space hungry but are relatively light. In order to accomplish the most efficient space usage these goods may be transported without the fibre filling or alternatively are vacuum packed. However, this operation then creates the need for additional work upon receipt to fill the cushions and unpacking of the vacuum packs as well as treating the product through pressing or steaming.

The transport of goods in cartons that eventually will be displayed on hangers, such as men's formal suits or ladies tailored garments, is done to maximise the space efficiency in containers. Upon arrival they will need to be unpacked and placed on hangers and will have to be steamed either with a hand steamer or pass through a steam tunnel. In most cases this will also require the attachment of price tickets and garment information labels.

Repackaging may be required where bulk transit quantities need to be debagged and repackaged into smaller stock room packs ready for allocation to stores.

It does happen that there may be garments received from the supplier with defects or returned from stores which are repairable in order to make them available in a saleable state which has to be done by the value-adder.

The location of the added value service provider can be either at an independent site or be incorporated in the retailer's warehouse facility. The challenge with an offsite location, particularly with the receipt of offshore product is the fact that the goods are received by another facility and reflect on a separate stock record which renders the administration of stock to be more complex.

It is preferable to have the value added processing done in the retailer's warehouse facility as there is control of the receipt of the goods and performance is more easily managed. The operation can possibly be done on a contractual basis whereby the processor rents space within the warehouse or the space is alternatively staffed with warehouse resources as a separate entity and not included in the distribution centre operational costs. It should be noted that the cost of this processing work forms part of the cost of the product and must be included in the determination of the product margin.

The costing structures for work done is a complex one as the type of work is not always consistent and therefore needs to be broken down into some detail.

Value added costing would typically consist of a basic cost for the overheads and handling of the product which is usually relatively stable but may vary depending on the type of product being processed. Charges per operation such as a rate per garment for steaming, labelling, placing on hangers and the like will be added to the base costs. Out of the ordinary operations such as ad hoc repairs will be dependent on the results of negotiation between the processor and the buying departments.

TRANSPORT METHODOLOGIES

The method of transport will be determined by a number of criteria. The option for clothing is either in cartons or in the form of hanging sets. The choice is dependent mainly on the characteristic of the product, the cost comparison between the two models and the equipment infra-structure of the supplier and distribution centres. Many of the more sophisticated production plants have the overhead rail systems that can accommodate hanging goods and which can facilitate the transport of the goods hanging from rails affixed to the ceiling of the vehicle to the retailer.

The cost of the hanging storage and transport of product will come at added expense for the rail systems in comparison to the charge for distribution in cartons. The time saving as a cost offset in the case of moving hanging goods needs to be considered and in many cases it is also dependent on the nature of fabrics such as voiles as well as the structure of garments as is the case for formal wear. If crease sensitive goods are moved in cartons there is a need for an added value processing requirement to steam and bag the goods which can either take place at the distribution centre or at the stores upon receipt which comes at an additional cost. The transport of formal wear in cartons could also lead to persistent creases in the garment such as the fold in pants that may be difficult to eradicate even with intense steaming.

Where retailers insist on receiving goods in boxes, a reverse cost may have to be applied where sophisticated manufacturing plants that only cater for hanging goods to maximise the scales of efficiency will need to purchase cartons and employ additional labour to pack the garments into boxes as well as encounter an additional time delay.

The downsides of the hanging format is that the equipment is expensive, space requirement is greater, and where multiple hangers are hung vertically to save space in the outer bag there could be the danger of bunching of longer garments at the bottom of the bag. Space wastage below the hanging bags in the vehicles also needs to be taken into account.

The advantage of time saving that hanging formats deliver in comparison to goods transported in cartons is that goods in cartons have the benefit of easier handling, better space utilization and less capital investment.

However the necessity of capacity planning for processing to steam and place products on hangers together with the additional cost, extended lead time and a risk that the quality may be compromised needs to be weighed up.

Another determining factor will be the aesthetics of the garment that may lend it to be displayed on hangers such as casual shirts made from natural fibres or styled tailored goods which will better highlight the features and promote the unique feel of the special fabrics.

Goods are stored and dispatched as hanging sets that will comprise of a fixed number of garments in the same colour and sizes and are allocated as such. This makes for easier handling and loading into vehicles especially where the equipment is able to access the vehicle or container directly from the despatch area.

The optimisation of the supply chain calls for an end to end cost analysis and monitoring to ensure that the goods reach the sales floors efficiently to best service the customer through consistent availability without the congestion of stock in warehouses and back rooms.

A flow diagram which indicates the garment and fibre types which best suit the method of storage, transport and display can be illustrated as follows

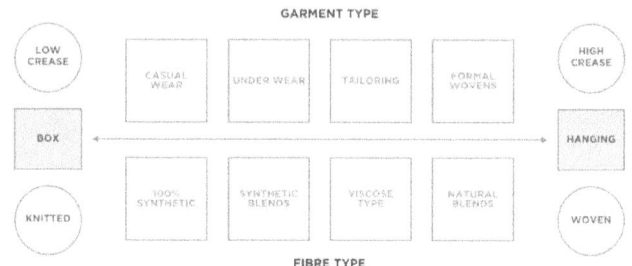

Product security

Wastage through pilferage is an important factor that needs attention during the movement of the product. Control is done by various methods but mostly through the use of sealed containers, marked sealing tapes on cartons, sample tests of contents in cartons, locked and sealed back doors on trucks and sophisticated handover procedures. There is a breakeven point where the cost to maintain the security must be weighed up against the shrinkage allowance as it may be overkill to secure cheaper products with refined protection. The additional labour and checkpoints will slow down the movement of product through the pipeline as well as lower the service levels and therefore may not make it meaningful. On the other hand it could well be very worthwhile for the movement of high value product.

Carton specifications and requirements

Transit and outer case cartons need to conform to certain specifications in terms of size, strength, weight, markings and sealing. The characteristics of certain products will dictate modifications to some cartons such as goods that are packed on hangers may require a tape at the ends inside the box to hook the hangers to prevent the shifting of product such as blouses within the cartons. Other products may require separators between the garments such as tissue paper or card board to minimise creasing.

Careful consideration must be given to the number of units per stockroom pack which will usually be by solid colour and solid size and should be equivalent to the unit of allocation. Savings can be achieved through less handling and storage configurations by setting the quantity per pack equivalent to the minimum allocation quantity that a store can accommodate without being overstocked.

Barcode markings enable the scanning in of boxes at the receipt points and alleviate the risk of congestion with less labour. Packing away on palettes into the storage slots is also done more quickly.

Markings on the cartons must be uniform and conform to international regulations and display a recognized certification stamp.

Side 1 marking required on the carton – product description

MARKING	DESCRIPTION
Retailer ABC	Name of the customer who is to take ownership of the product
Fragile	Indicates if the box should be handled with care
Supplier	Source of product where goods were supplied
Order no	Order that the box belongs to
Batch number	Production batch that carton belongs to
Product reference no	Style number of garments inside the box
SKU number	Stock keeping unit or barcode number that will be reflected on the stock records
Contents description	Style / colour / size and style description
Units per carton	Number of units inside the carton
Carton number	Number of carton out of the total (e.g. 'carton no 3 of 10')
Country of origin	Sending country (where carton was packaged)

Side 2 marking required on the carton – weight and measurement information

MARKING	DESCRIPTION
Fragile	Indicates if the box should be handled with care
Stack max	Maximum number of cartons that can be packed on top of each other
Net weight (kg)	Net weight in kg of goods inside the carton
Gross weight (kg)	Total weight of the outer carton and the goods inside the carton
Dimensions (cm or mm)	Dimensions of height, length and width of carton in cm or mm

Apart from conforming to international rules, the size parameters and volume dimensions will also be dictated by the pallette sizes and storage slots of the warehouse to safeguard the most efficient usage of space. The dimensions also need to be considered in terms of what the other equipment such as conveyer belts, vehicle capacities and store storage facilities can accommodate.

Carton critical measurements

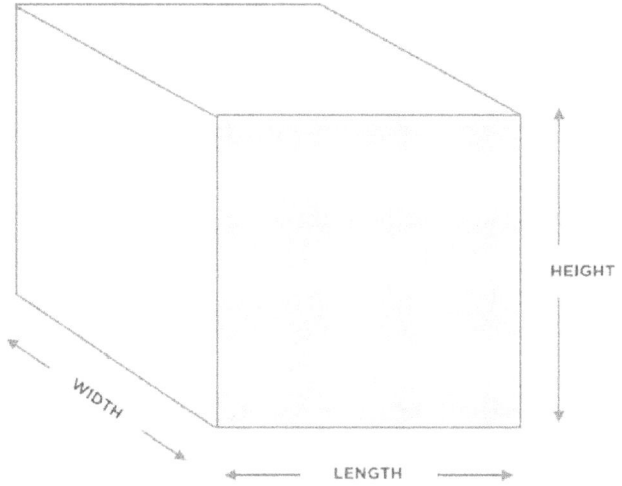

VOLUME = WIDTH X LENGTH X HEIGHT

Local logistics should investigate the possible use of returnable cartons or crates by suppliers much in the same way food retailers utilise lugs. Such an operation would be environmentally friendly and would incur a once off investment but the administration of such an operation does come at a cost which may influence the viability.

REVIEW AND ACTION OPTIONS OF TRADING IN SEASON

Process of comparing the actual performance in relation to the plan

No matter how much time and thought is spent in drafting the strategy and planning forecast it is inevitable that the reality will deviate from what is expected as a result of the volatile internal and external factors that exist at the time. Therefore it is critical to continually review actual performance, analyse the trends and take appropriate action to minimise the risks. Where adjustments are not able to be made to remedy a situation the lessons learnt must be taken on board and banked to be avoided in future trading seasons.

The path to follow in the process of comparing the actual performance in relation to the plan can be outlined as follows

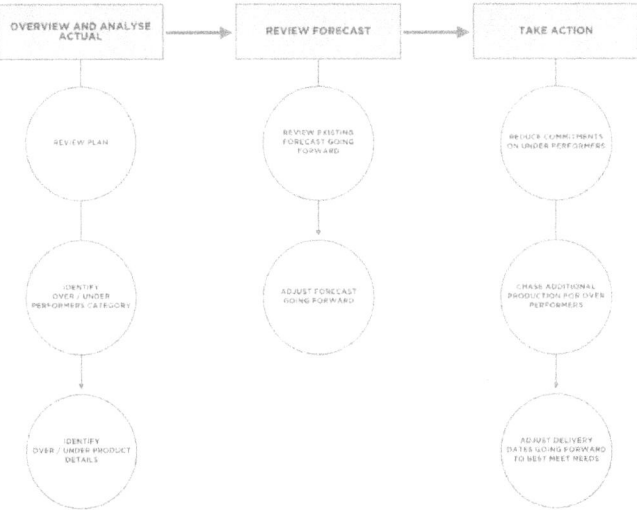

The start point of analysing and comparing the actual performance to the intended plan at a point in time, is to firstly to compare actual sales to date at total departmental level and drill down to product level and based on the result, review the planned sales for the balance of the season.

The potential new sales forecast is then compared to the actual commitment of product in the form of stock on hand at stores, product in transit and that at the supplier as well as the orders in the pipeline to determine the resultant shortage or surplus of stock.

In the scenarios below the assumption is that the department consists of a product which is over performing, another that is under performing and one that is selling to expectation.

The procedure which needs to be followed can be broken down into three distinct activities.

- The recording of the total plan for the season in terms of sales and the planned breaking stocks at the end of the season as well as the current week's performance which has just been completed.

- Based on the comparison of the actual sales to date in relation to that which was budgeted for may require a review of the balance of sales to be achieved and thereby create a revised forecast for the total season. The change in the sales forecast may also then require an adaptation of the planned breaking stocks to reflect the reality of the sales plan.
- Once the realistic revised sales performance has been established, the result then needs to be compared to the total stock commitment and assessed whether there is sufficient stock in the pipeline to achieve the revised targets. If this is not the case, a plan has to be devised in order to determine what action is required to achieve this or conversely there may be a consequent surplus of stock which will have to be reduced.

Analysis and adjustment of sales and commitment status tabulated in three focus areas

TOTAL SEASON STATUS AND CURRENT SALES

STYLE NO	DESCRIPTION	SELLING PRICE	LY SALES	TOTAL SEASON 26 WEEKS				END SEASON STOCKS		WEEK NO 6			
				SEASON BUDGET	% INC / DEC ON LY	REVISED SEASON F/CAST	% INC / DEC ON LY	BUDGET CLOSING STOCK	REVISED CLOSING STOCK	WEEKS LY SALES	WEEKS SALES BUDGET	WEEKS ACTUAL SALES	% INC / DEC ON LY
1234	Round neck t-shirt	99.99	950 000	1 100 500	15.8%	1 006 500	7.0%	180 000	150 000	35 000	42 500	43 000	11.4%
1235	V-neck t-shirt	120.99	940 000	1 150 000	16.2%	1 260 000	27.3%	250 000	200 000	38 000	43 200	45 500	18.4%
1236	Button down t-shirt	150	1 100 000	1 200 000	9.1%	1 210 000	10.0%	220 000	220 000	38 000	41 300	41 000	7.9%
	TOTAL DEPARTMENT		3 040 000	3 450 600	13.5%	3 486 500	14.7%	650 000	570 000	111 000	127 100	125 000	12.6%

PROGRESSIVE SALES STATUS

STYLE NO	DESCRIPTION	SELLING PRICE	6 WEEKS TO DATE							20 WEEKS BALANCE TO ACHIEVE				
			PROGRESS LY SALES TO DATE	PROGRESS BUDGET SALES TO DATE	% INC / DEC ON LY	ACTUAL PROGRESS SALES TO DATE	% INC / DEC ON LY	PROGRESS REVISED SALES TO DATE	% INC / DEC ON LY	BALANCE OF LY SALES	BALANCE OF BUDGET SALES TO ACHIEVE	% INC / DEC ON LY	REVISED BALANCE OF SALES TO ACHIEVE	% INC / DEC ON LY
1234	Round neck t-shirt	99.99	190 000	220 000	15.8%	205 000	7.9%	219 000	10.5%	760 000	880 500	15.9%	811 500	6.8%
1235	V-neck t-shirt	120.99	250 000	290 500	16.2%	318 000	27.2%	300 000	20.0%	740 000	859 600	16.2%	942 000	27.3%
1236	Button down t-shirt	150	235 000	250 505	6.6%	252 000	7.2%	252 000	7.2%	865 000	949 495	9.8%	958 000	10.8%
	TOTAL DEPARTMENT		675 000	761 005	12.7%	775 000	14.8%	762 000	12.9%	2 365 000	2 689 595	127 100	2 711 500	14.7%

COMMITMENT STATUS

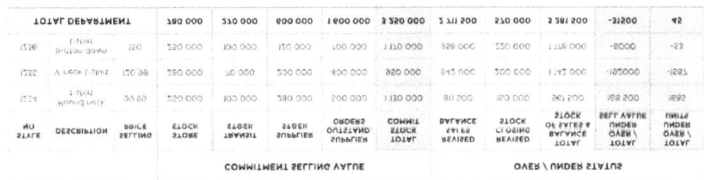

STYLE NO	DESCRIPTION	SELLING PRICE	COMMITMENT SELLING VALUE						SALES / ORDERS GIVEN			
			STOCK ON ORDER	TRANSIT STOCK	STORES STOCK	TOTAL COMMITTED PURCHASES	COMMIT STOCK ON SALES	BALANCE TO REALIZE	STOCK TO REALIZED	TOTAL ORDER GIVEN ON ORDER	TOTAL ORDER GIVEN ON STOCK	TOTAL ORDER GIVEN SALES
1234	Round neck t-shirt	99.99	520 000	100 000	580 000	200 000	1 320 000	811 200	150 000	961 200	968 200	1892
1235	V-neck t-shirt	150.98	580 000	10 000	530 000	400 000	920 000	945 000	300 000	1 245 000	-185000	-1285
1236	Button down t-shirt	120	520 000	100 000	150 000	100 000	1 110 000	928 000	150 000	1 018 000	-8000	-22
	TOTAL DEPARTMENT		180 000	530 000	800 000	1 900 000	3 520 000	3 311 200	210 000	2 381 200	-21200	42

Logically speaking based on the tabular representation above of the scenarios, the thought process may well progress as follows.

Scenario 1: Style 1234 round neck t-shirt selling for 99.99 currently has an original season's budget of 1,100,500 which represents a 15.8% increase on last year. Based on the actual performance during the past six weeks the budget is set at a value of 220,000 that still represents a 15.8% where in fact the actual 6 weeks have performed to a value of 205,000 which is only 7.9%. Based on this fact the reviewer then thinks that going forward for the balance of the season a potential increase of 6.8% is more probable than the 15.9% originally planned. Adjustment to the revised level will result the total season being 1,016,500 rather than the 1,100,500 originally anticipated. At the same time the view on the breaking stock is that it will be 150,000 based on the reduced sales for the balance of the season rather than the original plan of 180,000. Thus the stock requirement to complete the sales to the end of the season as well as meet the revised closing stock need means the amount of stock necessary is 961,500. However, when the actual stock in stores, stock in transit, and stock at the supplier as well as outstanding orders still planned to be produced totals 1,130,000 it is clear to see that there is a surplus of 168,500 which at a selling price of 99.99 translates into 1685 units. Action is required to deal with this over commitment. Options are described later on in this section.

Scenario 2: Style 1235 v neck t-shirt selling for 120.99 currently has an original season's budget of 1,150,100 which represents a 16.2% increase on last year. Based on the actual performance during the past six weeks there have been revisions to a value of 300,000 that represents a good 20.0%, however the actual 6 weeks have over performed to a value of 318,000 which is 27.2%. The reviewer then thinks that going forward for the balance of the season an increase of 27.3% is therefore more probable than the 16.2% originally planned which will result in the total season being 1,260,000 rather than the 1,150,100 originally anticipated. At the same time the view on the breaking stock is that it will be 200,000 based on the higher sales going forward will erode stocks and will be less than the original plan of 250,000. The stock requirement to complete the sales to the end of the season and to meet the revised closing stock need means the amount of stock required is 1,142,000. However when the actual stock in stores, stock in transit, and stock at the supplier as well as outstanding orders still planned to be produced it is clear to see that there is a shortfall of 192,000 which at a selling price of 120.99 translates into a deficit of 1587 units. Action is required to deal with this under commitment.

Scenario 3: Style 1236 Button down t-shirt. In this scenario the same process as followed in scenarios 1 and 2 delivers the result that the style performed closely to what was planned and was only 53 units short of target which therefore resulted in no need for any action.

Analysis options

Before deciding on what action is required there are consistent questions that need to be answered. In terms of why the sales differ to the plan one needs to determine whether the sales were early or late possibly due to seasonal factors or extraordinary events. However if they are low the question must be asked whether it is because the appeal to the customer is below expectation.

Measurement against key targets should also be considered as well as the guidelines that are outlined in the strategy. The proportions of the customer segmentation may be incorrectly projected. The pricing policy such as price tiering could be incorrectly balanced, new initiatives may be over optimistic or colour trends are not be as expected and therefore the deviation should be examined down to the lowest level of the hierarchy.

Key performance measures to focus on are forward cover targets to confirm that they are in line or if they are too low the reason may be that there is not enough stock in the system to enable achievement of targeted sales. The measures at store level need to be evaluated as the bigger selling stores may be significantly impacting sales if their individual targets are not being achieved.

Sell off percentage which is defined as the total stock received divided by sales expressed as a percentage, is often used as a key measure but a word of caution is that this needs to carefully assessed as sales with low stocks may deliver a flattering result that leaves a lot better impression than deserved or conversely a disappointing sell off percentage of a product may be due to a full delivery having been received in the latter part of the period and therefore the opportunity to sell was restricted. The value that this measurement has is only truly valid when all products being measured are for the same period of time when full stocks were in place and then can be used as a fair relativity measure between products or to the comparable acceptable levels of sell off.

It is key that all planned promotions and deliveries are still in line to be launched as scheduled and that there are no risks of late or non-delivery from the supplier as this will impact on performance for the balance of the season.

Historical comparison must be considered carefully especially in the case where events fall differently in that this year they may fall on the weekend instead of a week day as may have been the case in the previous year. Special events unique to the season could also have a significant effect. Much of this type of insight is gained through regular store and supplier visits, as well as strict adherence to meeting schedules that include all of the stakeholders comprising of buyers, merchandisers, allocators, designers and technologists. Working as a team keeps everyone involved and committed to an action plan complete with assignments and timelines and a system of updates that monitor the progress of action items.

Differing trends or patterns to that expected may have evolved such as prints which may emerge to be in higher demand than plains.

The review of better selling products as well as the worst sellers needs to be analytically done in an attempt to understand as to why they are performing as they are. Factors that may be common are styling features, colourations, functionality or fabrications. Styles programmed going forward should be reviewed for the identification of opportunities to adapt or change, move out or pull forward and if possible turn on or cancel production.

Regular probes on the sales floor and interaction with sales staff and customers often reveal obvious reasons which are commonly overlooked particularly when one is, as is typical, too close to the detail. Customer focus groups can also provide valuable comprehensions into the practical needs of the consumers and highlight opportunities where sales can be improved and poor quality issues may be exposed.

Action options

In scenario 1 the various possibilities should be considered where action is needed to reduce the commitment in order to minimise potential markdowns.

The stage of completion of the outstanding orders must be determined and if the fabric has yet to be cut, an immediate hold should be put on the order. It is preferable to be left with uncut fabric than with made up garments. The fabric can possibly be converted into other areas of need and be made up in faster selling styles if it is appropriate. Fabric can be held over to be incorporated into a future season's programme if suitable but if it is not right, the last resort would be to sell the fabric off and take the loss on the fabric alone.

Outstanding orders or made up goods at suppliers may need, where possible, to move out the delivery dates or alternatively cancel unmade orders. A point to note is that this decision may require sensitive negotiations with the supplier's in order that they fully understand reasoning and it is encouraged that the resolution of the situation becomes a collaboration of problem solving.

The sales performance at individual store level should be carefully analysed and where there are stores that are selling the product at acceptable levels, that stock is moved from underperforming stores to those where there is a likelihood of improved sell offs. When this is considered as an option it is important to weigh up the cost of the relocation of the product against the possibility of clearing the goods at an acceptable rate. If it is deemed not to be workable it should not be done. Where the product is not in all stores, the temptation is often to extend the catalogue in the hope that the goods may be cleared through greater exposure. This may, however simply spread the problem so should be contemplated with great caution.

A successful strategy could possibly be to launch a promotion and sell the goods at a discounted price in whatever form. The practice may be a simple price reduction, a "two for one" campaign or special discount offers to loyalty programme members.

If all else fails, the last resort is to remove the product from display as it is possibly clogging saleable space and hold back from allocating any stock at the supplier and wait for the major seasonal sale launch to clear the goods. What is essential is that it needs to be clearly understood as to why the product was not wanted and bank the lessons for future seasons to ensure the errors are not repeated.

In the scenario 2 the net result showed that there was a shortfall of required stock due to over performance and the action required would enable the maximisation of the opportunities to achieve additional sales.

The first investigation that should take place is to see whether additional product can be turned on which is dependent on the availability of fabric, components and production capacity. The possibility of converting slower selling styles planned for the balance of the season is frequently a feasible option. Any existing outstanding orders should be pulled forward and the gap that evolves be replaced with the turn on orders. A word of warning is that while the temptation exists to turn on product it is critical that the delivery timeline will allow the full achievement of potential additional sales. If the delivery is too close to the end of the trading period particularly in the case of seasonal product it may result in the product landing up on the reduced counter and thereby eradicating the benefit of extra profits.

The analysis of sales at store level may reveal that certain stores are underperforming in relation to other stores and therefore the catalogue could be reduced to ensure continuity of stock in those stores that are delivering above average sales.

In the same light as the identification of the unique feature of the underperforming product, it is equally important to understand the features that can be attributed to the good performance of other products and put on file for future referral.

POST SEASON TRADE ANALYSIS

A key focus in the assessment of the past performance for the season is to compare the actual key numbers to that what was expected and understand the deviations whether they were positive or negative. The learnings are imperative in the compilation of a new season's strategy and setting of targets.

The key topics that need to be questioned and evaluated are:

Product

- Were the trends which were anticipated in line with what actually materialised? What needs to be taken into account when predicting the future season's trends?
- Did the strategy that was set for the brand and customer together with that of the group and department as well as the supplier selection deliver the envisaged objectives? What needs to be done differently for the new season?

Customers and competitors

- Did the information on customer segmentation and the action plans cater effectively in the satisfaction of the needs? What adaptations and additional resources are needed for the future season?
- Did the competitor initiatives which were anticipated actually happen and was it possible to effectively counteract them? What other methodologies are available to keep up to date with the market place activities?

Key performance Indicators

- Were the targets of sales, margins, stock levels and turns, gross and net profits achieved as per plan or were they unrealistic? What measures require review and which activities are needed to be put in place to achieve them in the new season?
- Was the product assortment in the right proportions and did they perform to acceptable levels to cater for all customer segments

effectively? Were the product innovations and promotions that were implemented successful and at the right levels?
- What were the actual colours and sizes sold in comparison to the volumes purchased and what should have been bought instead?
- Identify product sales which need to be adjusted to a realistic level as a result of product failure, poor availabilities and any other factors such as competitive activity and what special events were there that may have influenced sales either positively or negatively.

Suppliers
- Did the suppliers perform to the levels that maximised availability in the right quantities and on time?
- Did the selected suppliers possess the right capabilities to deliver the programmes that were allotted in terms of innovation, complexity, capacity, quality and on time delivery? Are there other suppliers who should be considered?
- Was the feedback received from suppliers of a nature that can help improve the working relationships going forward?

Stores
- Were stores able to understand the structure of the ranges and easily display them to emphasize the thinking of the buying team? What improvements to guidelines can be made to assist them?

- Was the feedback received from stores valuable and what mechanisms can be implemented to improve the quality of feedback?

Marketing

- Were the marketing channels that were utilised effective and was the uplift in sales able to be measured accurately against control products? Which other communication mediums would be considered?
- Were the promotions successful and what was the extent of substitution purchases?
- What was the feedback from store staff and customers?
- Were the social initiative objectives achieved?

CONCLUSION

Up to now the book has tried to adequately describe in the main the principles and theory to follow in order to logically embark on the journey, perform the key activities and utilise the mechanisms involved in the complex retail network required from conceptualisation stage right through to presenting it to the customer as an offer to purchase.

There are however crucial elements of stewardship required to guarantee that the future is both successful and sustainable. The demonstration of those elements which are characteristic to a true merchant are outlined below.

Integrity is an absolute unconditional prerequisite that should be evident in all the interactions with all stake holders. In short it is important to uphold the promise of doing what you say you are going to do and maintain a policy of under promising and over delivering.

Passion is clearly illustrated through attributes such as the visible demonstration of the love for the organisation, the product and relationships in such a way that it is contagious and serves as a great motivator to all those who come in contact with a sincere energised trader. An underlying sense of urgency to cope with the continual changes that the marketplace pitches at the retail participants. The response to such events whether they originate from the customers or other competitors needs to be such that it remains composed and the analysis of the situation prepares a clear path of creative action to withstand such onslaughts.

Humility is demonstrated through the focussed retailer from all levels of seniority who listens to customer and sales staff feedback and opinions with an enquiring mind and courteously probes and takes heed of their comments. Often there is a temptation to arrogantly brush disagreeable criticisms aside as being irrelevant but this should be avoided at all costs and every effort should be made to seek to understand and apply different thought processes. This is especially evident in this day and age where the social media has become an indispensable part of day to day living where something that was thought to be initially insignificant can in a matter of hours demand full attention and therefore the need to be sensitive to outside inputs is intensified.

Vigilance and alertness is a precondition to keep the finger on the pulse. An example of this is in the same way that the customer is the reason for the existence of the retailer so are the competitors in a way. The retailer needs to know their rivals intimately and keep watch on them like a hawk. It is so often easy to treat the smaller minnow contestants with contempt and scoff at any hint of threat. However it should be remembered that there are many success stories of such upstart retailers that have rattled the foundations of well-established traders, some of whom are today no more than romantic memories of the past. It is therefore important to admire the boldness of new and emerging entrants and possibly learn from the courageous innovations that many bring with them as they make their way up the ladder in the industry. In the same way there are other competitors who are on the way down the ladder and from them there are many lessons to be learnt as to why they are in decline. In essence therefore the competitors have a valuable input into the sustainability of their counterparts.

Partnerships between the retailer and the supplier is an essential pre-requisite to ensure the success of the retailer. There has to be a circle of trust to promote collaboration and mutual respect. As has been highlighted the only guarantee about change is that there will be change and it is without doubt that the retailers' greatest ally when change happens, whether it be positive or negative, is their source of supply. The support of the supplier through their flexibility and ability to appreciate the need for revolution is vital for the shared destiny and the celebration of success for both businesses through maintaining healthy relationships with the customer.

Complacency is probably the greatest enemy of the retailer, particularly those who are enjoying great trading performance or who have been a major player for many years and with it often comes an air of arrogance as well as a belief of invincibility. It is therefore critical to be obsessed with trying to keep one step ahead of the market through the deliverance of continual innovations, being open to new opportunities and supporting the reinvention of operations. If this is not maintained but rather the belief is taken steadfastly that the position is rock steady and stores are consequently allowed to deteriorate to a stage where they look old and tired. Similarly if the merchandise is allowed to become much of the same old same old it is inevitable that dwindling sales figures will reflect the result of such complacency. The sad thing is that by the time that the alarm bells are rung, the damage may already be done and the sales rate suddenly does not support the investment required to fix the situation. The more likely solutions which are applied in an attempt to salvage the situation are to dramatically cut costs of anything and everything which in turn inhibits any rejuvenation initiatives and the implementation of staff retrenchment drives not only adds to the burden to those who are left behind but also does irreparable damage to morale. The tactic to increase profit margins in order to generate additional income is often seen as the saving grace but this is in turn is frequently rejected by the consumer who is now being asked to pay more probably for less appealing product in very ordinary facilities which results in her crossing the road to explore alternative options.

In summary, having a farsighted view of the overall big picture of the retail environment, with an all-inclusive attention to detail and being aware of early warning signs to effectively avoid challenges through the optimised use of the tools, mechanisms and talents at hand is without doubt a key factor in delivering a successful and sustainable retail business.

INDEX

A

B

C

Referrals and acknowledgements

Akhil Jk: (2015) *Fashion Technology for Supervisors*

Bob Phibbs: (2010) *The Retail Doctor's guide to growing your business*, John Wiley & Sons, New Jersey

Business Plan Expert: (2014) *Fashion Business Plan Template,* Liraz Publishing

Meir Liraz: (2013) *Guide to Effective Retail Merchandise Management – a step by step guide to Merchandising in a Retail Store,* Liraz Publishing

DMS Retail: (2012) *Retail Math Made Simple,* DMS Retail Inc.,

Doug Stephens: (2013) *The Retail Revival: Reimagining business for the new age of consumerism,* John Wiley & Sons, Canada

Steve Hayes, John McLoughlin and Dorothy Fairclough: (2012) *Cooklins Garment*

Technology for Fashion Designers, John Wiley & Sons, United Kingdom

Sarah Hayward: *Fashion Blogging: How to Become a Superstar Fashion Blogger*

Michelle Sackson: (2014) *The Ultimate Guide to Starting a Clothing Line,* K&K Publishing

Tim Jackson, David Shaw: (2001) *Mastering fashion buying & merchandising management,* Palgrave Macmillan

Keith Bartlett: (2013) *The Internal Supply Chain of the Retailer*

Keith Bartlett: (2013) *Inventory Accuracy at Store Level*

Rosemary Varley: (2014) *Retail Product Management Buying and merchandising,* Routledge

Judi Bevan: (2001) *The rise and fall of Marks & Spencer,* Profile Books Ltd

Tony Owen – Thank you for your valuable input and advice

Renee Nesbitt – Thank you for the diagram and tabular layouts

www.ingramcontent.com/pod-product-compliance
Lightning Source LLC
Chambersburg PA
CBHW051445170526
45166CB00001B/121